2013 N
ME
Exemplary Christian Education
Book Award

Unraveling the Christmas Star Mystery has been awarded the Gold Medal as the 2013 Exemplary Christian Education Book.

The Illumination Book Award, sponsored by the Jenkins Group, was designed to honor and bring increased recognition to the year's best Christian Education title written and published with a Christian worldview.

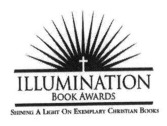

Unraveling the
CHRISTMAS
STAR *Mystery*

Validation of the Holy Bible

IRENE BARON

Irene J Baron

Dedication

This book is dedicated to those seeking validation of the Christmas star event.

Contents

Illustrations

Acknowledgments

I wish to thank the Educator Resource Center, Space Center Houston, National Aeronautics & Space Administration for the sixty-eight mathematically precise astronomy computer programs used in the successful research to locate the Christmas star.

The John McIntire Library team of reference librarians were phenomenal in locating numerous requested reference books. They facilitated my historical studies concerning celestial symbols and associated symbolic interpretations used by astronomers of ancient civilizations preceding the birth of Jesus Christ.

This research and subsequent discovery of the Christmas star event would have been impossible without the availability and mathematical computations of computers. Thank you Apple Inc. and International Business Machines Corporation.

Many thanks and much appreciation to my daughter, Dominique Baron, who provided encouragement through my writing processes.

Illustration by Irene Baron

Introduction

NASA (National Aeronautics & Space Administration) provided sixty-eight mathematically precise astronomy computer programs for use with my high school astronomy classes in Earth Science. Written by mathematicians and scientists, the programs were so diverse they could be used to track **celestial** motions of the Sun, Moon, **Planet**s and stars in many different ways.

I loved teaching with the computer programs and using my home computer to learn more about astronomy. My students were in awe of the technology being provided to them. They had access to them during classes and study halls. It was a win-win situation!

The first thing that came to my mind while surveying the programs was a question. Could these multiple astronomy programs tell me what happened in the sky when Jesus Christ was born? Could I prove there really was a Christmas star? If so, what was it?

Past speculation for the physical explanation of the Christmas star included that it was a comet, an exploding star called a **nova** or **supernova**, or a **conjunction** of planets. A conjunction of planets is when the planets appear to merge in the sky. Since planet **orbital** paths are millions of miles apart in their distance from the Sun, they don't physically meet. Were any of these the Christmas star? Legends about the Christmas star and events surrounding the birth of **Jesus** Christ have generated stories, myths, and speculation. I wanted to find the truth.

I always enjoyed searching for information. Before the advent of computers I used books. Now, I could use mathematically precise astronomy programs. The movements of the Sun, Moon, planets and stars in the sky don't change their patterns of motion, so the computer programs would be accurate. To have the opportunity to find out about the celestial objects of 2000-years ago was going to be a fun challenge. I loved challenges. I was going to find out if there really was a Christmas star.

Did I find out what happened? I sure did!

It was an exciting journey back into history, for not only did I have to find the event set which was predicted and anticipated by the ancient scientists (called **astronomers**, astrologers, **cosmologists**, **magi**, **magicians**, **priests**, or wisemen), I had to learn about that time in history. How did the ancients interpret the symbols of what they saw in the sky? What was symbolic to them? Why would they use the event of some celestial happening to predict the birth of the greatest God to be born in the universe?

Information about the manner in which ancient astronomers interpreted motions of celestial objects has been gathered over the years by historians and archaeologists. They used evidence from ancient buildings and temples with statues, wall carvings and paintings, pictures, stories written in stone, and ancient documents found in Asia, China, and throughout the Middle East.[1]

During my studies of almost 100-books on ancient history, archeology, and art, I learned that astronomers of 2000-years ago used dawn as the time of day for their celestial observations.

This was very important fact to know. Most past researchers seeking to find the Christmas star had used early evening as the time for their searches. To be accurate, calculations during the computer searches were set for dawn in the local time zone of Bethlehem while using the correct latitude and longitude for that location. I consistently used six o'clock in the morning.

It is important for you to know the differences between "astronomers" who scientifically study all that is beyond Earth, "astrologers" who believe positions of objects in the sky influence humankind, and of "cosmologists" who are philosophers trying to explain how the universe originated and exists.

Astrology in ancient Greece referred to those talking about the stars, or using star talk. "Aster" is a prefix meaning "star" while "logos" refers to speech. In contrast, the "nomos" in the word astronomy derives from "law." Thus astronomy can be interpreted to mean "starlaw".[2] Astronomy is based on fact.

The astronomers of two thousand years ago used astrology to explain the movements of all celestial bodies. Following the laws of nature, the precise movements of all objects within the universe have continued since the theoretical big bang, the beginning of the universe as we know it.

The Big Bang Theory was finally adopted by the Catholic church. In 1951, Pope Pius XII gave a speech before the Pontifical Academy of Sciences with reference to the Big Bang theory stating: "…it would seem that present-day science, with one sweep back across the centuries, has succeeded in bearing witness to the august instant of the primordial Fiat Lux [Let there be Light], when along with matter, there burst forth from nothing a sea of light and radiation, and the elements split and churned and formed into millions of galaxies." The Internet website address of the entire speech for interested readers is: http://www.papalencyclicals.net/Pius12/P12EXIST.HTM

A Christian would state that God set the wheels in motion for everything to happen at the correct time and place in the future at the moment of creation. Termed a miracle by some, the largest birth announcement in the history of mankind occurred at a time when it could be observed, interpreted, and understood.

The statement in the Holy Bible, Galatians 4:41: "But when the fullness of the time was come, God sent forth His Son," tells us that His Son would be born when everything was perfect for that event. And it was. At that time in history, the known world was at a peace enforced by the Roman armies. People could travel safely and did. That peace enabled the wisemen with their astronomers and entourages to travel from their homelands to Bethlehem in Judea.

Ancient astronomers erroneously believed every object existing in the sky was a god. In addition, their interpretations of this celestial birth announcement told that the new God would be the most powerful God in the universe. This was going to be a God who would change their way of thinking and the religions of the world. The wisemen became, perhaps, the first gentiles to worship him.

Included in this book are explanations of events occurring within several months leading up to Christ's birth and which ancient astronomers foretold using their mathematical calculations of celestial observations. At that time in history, leaders of some ruling bodies on Earth had been informed by their astronomers that these future celestial events symbolized not only the birth of the greatest God to ever exist, but the first true God to be born on Earth.

The ancient astronomers, like those of today, were some of the most brilliant persons alive. Astronomers of 2,000 to 4,000-years ago, the most knowledgeable men in their nations, empires or kingdoms, would have been prime counselors to the rulers.[2] When celestial events transpired, the rulers were informed what the related symbolisms meant and what action should be taken.

Celestial events could be predicted as far back as Babylonian times, 4,000-years ago.[3] Written **Chinese** astronomical records began with the Bronze Age, over 3,000-years ago. All mathematical calculations at that time in history were completed with the **abacus** or by hand, taking much labor and time.

A brilliant exploding star, a supernova, has often been an erroneous explanation for the Christmas star. Supernovae have been spotted periodically with 2011 A.D. being a record year of discoveries. Such supernovae continue to be celebrated around the globe by present day astronomers.[4] To illustrate the importance of exploding stars and the impact they have had on humans, I include information about a famous one from the past.

In 1054 A.D. a star too far away to be seen by the naked eye exploded and became visible due to the growing brilliance. Since it was previously not visible, witnesses thought it was a "nova", a new star. Any star that experiences thermonuclear explosions at its surface and rapidly expands in brightness is called a nova. Massive stars explode to become supernova stars so bright they can be seen from Earth during daylight hours.

The Chinese were inspired to seriously study astronomy beginning with the 1054 event. The 1054 written records from astronomer Yang Wei-te record that he prostrated himself before the Emperor and the court to report that a "guest star" had appeared with a faint yellow glow above it. Yang Wei-te interpreted this to mean that a person of great wisdom and virtue was in the country.

The fact that one lone star would signify so much, one thousand years after the birth of Jesus Christ, points out the importance attributed to celestial events in more ancient times.

The current shape of that particular nova is pictured above. Remaining centrally located matter of the 1054 nova eventually became a **neutron** star that is currently in the midst of a mass of glowing, expanding gases now called the Crab Nebula. This nebula can be seen above the southern horn of the bull in the constellation Taurus. Gases have been traveling outward from the center of that explosion at a measured rate of over 1400-kilometers per second.

The resulting Crab Nebula was rediscovered in 1731 by John Bevis, an English doctor and amateur astronomer. He brought it to the attention of the French astronomer, Charles Messier.

Messier, finding it confusing and difficult to study galaxies and nebulae by their multitude of proper names, assigned them numbers. He placed the nebula resulting from the 1054 supernova into his famous catalogue of clusters and nebulae as the first entry, naming it Messier 1, or M1. Since Messier began the numbering system, all galaxies are identified with the Messier or "M" designation and a following number. You will therefore find the Crab Nebula also found as M1. The current full color appearance of the much photographed Crab Nebula can be found with a quick Internet image search.

Ancient Japanese and Arabian writings also tell of the same "new star". Some archaeologists attribute early American Indian petroglyph drawings found in New Mexico and Arizona in the United States to the 1054 explosion. They illustrate a bright star next to the crescent Moon. Computer programs verify the Moon would have been in that alignment and phase as both objects rose at dawn that day.

The brightness of the 1054 explosion kept it visible to the naked eye for almost two years. For a few weeks it must have rivaled the brilliance of the planet Venus, a planet so bright it has sometimes cast a shadow.

Such star explosions as nova and supernova leave behind a remaining neutron star surrounded by an expanding, burning, gas cloud caused by the explosion. Analysis and measurement of the cloud expansion rate can give astronomers the approximate date of the original explosion.[5] Due to the fact there are no physical, nebulous remnants of any exploding star dating to the time of Christ's birth, it can be assumed the Christmas star was NOT a nova or supernova.

If one star could create such speculation, such as the one causing the Crab Nebula, the importance of the many different celestial events that occurred during the several months prior to Christ's birth must have created absolute wonder in the eyes of knowledgeable beholders. **Asians**, Chinese, **Egyptians**, Indians, and **Persians** all believed that such phenomenon meant the birth of a very great god who would dwell on Earth among men.

As a matter of protocol, great kingdoms would have sent an emissary to welcome the new God. This personage would have been someone of great importance in the kingdom, if not the ruler himself. They would not have traveled as a solitary man, but most likely with guards for protection. Servants, cooks, baggage carriers, beasts of burden, clothing, hardware, attendants, gifts, and all that was necessary to allow the emissary to travel in the splendid comfort befitting their station in life would have been part of their entourage.

The past extravagant religious rituals within their individual homelands had to have been considered minor compared to the planned meeting with the one true, living God. We can only imagine the preparations that took place by the emissaries chosen to embark from different countries on the journeys to the birthplace of Jesus Christ. They had been placed in a position where they had to take an extensive journey to welcome the God of the universe while representing their home country. What gifts they chose to offer had to be equal in magnificence to the new and very important God and the magnitude of the event. The situation must have created tumultuous times and much anxiety. The details, logistics, and protocol to be followed must have been argued and discussed for several years prior to the actual departures of the emissaries and their entourages toward Bethlehem.

To understand the celestial events that happened, it is advisable to review basic knowledge of astronomy, archeology, cosmology, and how they were practiced at the time of Jesus Christ.

The following illustration shows the location of the Crab Nebula (M1) in the sky. Through a telescope it will appear as a hazy area. Like many beautiful celestial phenomenon, using a clock drive on the telescope to counteract the Earth's rotation and a camera with a time exposure attached to the telescope viewfinder, anyone can take a picture of the nebula. Without the correct equipment, readers may locate a nearby astronomy club and avid local astronomers who will be anxious to assist them in their quest.

Through a love of learning and the advent of mathematically precise computer programs, the events creating the greatest birth announcement in the history of mankind have been discovered by a Christian.

INTRODUCTION:1 CRAB NEBULA

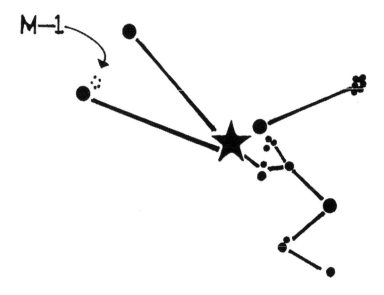

The position of the Crab Nebula (M1) is in the constellation of Taurus near the constellation Auriga. By aligning a telescope at the above illustrated M1 position you should see the nebula.

CHAPTER 1
Biblical Records

Holy Bible. King James Version. Luke 2:8-11:

8 And there were in the same country shepherds abiding in the field, keeping watch over their flock by night. 9 And, lo, the angel of the Lord came upon them, and the glory of the Lord shone round about them: and they were sore afraid. 10 And the angel said unto them, Fear not: for, behold, I bring you good tidings of great joy, which shall be to all people. 11 For unto you is born this day in the city of David a Savior, which is Christ the Lord.

Night is currently thought of that time in the twenty-four hour solar day cycle as an hour or so after sunset. Darkness appears and lasts until the twilight of dawn. When ancient astrologers used the words "night," they referred to the eve of the day or the night before.[1] That the Christmas angel said, "this day" informs us that it was after midnight and before the dawn.

If the angel would have said, "Unto you is born this night ...," we might consider the event had taken place in the evening before the midpoint of night, midnight. Before dawn was the time of day the astronomers of the pre-Christian era began to prepare for their most important celestial observations.

The Greek phrase, "in the east" translates to an object "rising before the Sun." This would be at dawn when astronomical observations took place. It can logically be concluded that the birth of Jesus Christ took place in the early morning hours, before dawn. The wisemen were following a morning event.

The celestial events announcing the birth of Jesus Christ culminated on the date of His birth over Bethlehem. Christians believe it was no coincidence that the events to signal and announce His birth were easily recognized by people in that time period in a manner they would comprehend. Those who understood the movements of the Sun, Moon, and stars were perhaps overwhelmed with what they found. The significance of the events would have been understood with the resulting symbolism and interpretations using the astrology and cosmology that had been handed down for centuries since the time of the Babylonians.

Led by astronomers, there was more than one set of recorded entourages following the morning star events to Bethlehem. Being important personages in their own right, each emissary most likely followed royal or official protocols of their homelands. They would therefore stop at residences of the reigning rulers to pay respect as they passed through the different regions.

Upon entering Herods' city at that time they would have found it had a usual population of around forty-thousand citizens with tents and temporary dwellings around the perimeter increasing that number. During the required census at that time, the large number of returnees would have greatly swelled that population.

It was within this area that Herod had his palace built with over 58,000-square feet of space. According to ancient writings, his temple was a beautiful building with extensive stone carvings and paintings within the stucco of flowers and geometric figures. Anyone entering the city would assume Herods life style matched the palace, being expansive and expensive. It was evidently a time of great wealth for the Romans and high taxes for the residents.

The emissaries probably assumed that King Herod, as the reigning authority, would have at his disposal not only intellectuals observing heavenly events, but would be on top of it all by pinpointing the actual location of the birth of the new God. It was assumed Herod's court advisors had been aware of the incredible celestial events and alerted Herod. They had not been aware and not alerted Herod.

The traveling emissaries must have pondered very seriously the interpretations to be made when their omnipotent gods omitted Herod and his followers from that sphere of knowledge. Why would Herod and those in his domain have been blinded to the information of the new God's birth? Was there a heavenly reason for Herod's ignorance? The only logical interpretation would have been that Herod's ignorance had been to protect the child God. The emissaries may have theorized that Herod must therefore be left in his state of ignorance.

What kingdom had not known jealous rulers and protectorates doing away with the lives of those who might challenge them? Herod's ignorance of such an event may have been manifested in his fear. Throughout history man has shown a habitual pattern of either ridiculing or fearing what he does not understand. Unfortunately, history also shows that fear of the strange, different, or the unknown often ends with violence. Having murdered three of his ambitious sons, Herod would easily have had the infant God killed.

Holy Bible. King James Version. Matthew, Chapter 2:1-3:

**1 Now when Jesus was born in Bethlehem
of Judaea in the days of Herod the king,
behold, there came wisemen from the east to
Jerusalem, 2 Saying, Where is He that is born
king of the Jews? For we have seen His star
in the east, and are come to worship Him. 3
When Herod the king had heard these things,
he was troubled, and all Jerusalem with him.**

National leaders usually try to rule wisely. In return, they receive great wealth and honors of the position and appreciate them.

Several visiting dignitaries from other lands converged at Herod's location and stopped to pay their respects. Passing through on a common mission, they surely wished to replenish their supplies. They explained they were going to pay homage and witness for themselves the God King being born within Herods realm.

The knowledge these emissaries possessed convinced Herod they were telling the truth. Herod showed no interest in following the stars to see the newborn God for himself. Instead he requested the emissaries to stop back and tell him the location of the child so that he could then honor the new God King, all the while plotting to kill Him. The Romans would want no new kings in Judea.

If a present day dictator would learn that a new king had just been born in his country to perhaps usurp him, he may be troubled. In Herods time, to have entourages representing other countries appear with the same startling news had been worrisome. Killing a new king would have been cheaper and safer than sending the royal born into exile.

Holy Bible. King James Version. Matthew 2:4-6:

4 And when he had gathered all the chief priests and scribes of the people together, he demanded of them where Christ should be born. 5 And they said unto him, In Bethlehem of Judea: for thus it is written by the prophet, 6 And thou Bethlehem, in the land of Judea, art not least among the princes of Judea: for out of thee shall come a governor, that shall rule my people Israel.

Herod, in all probability, retreated from the traveling dignitaries to speak with his advisors. By then, all local citizens of Jerusalem had heard of the emissaries and their God child quest, for their elegant entourages would have invaded the city to fill water jars, buy food, and resupply their caravans. Their strange clothing and languages would have alerted anyone they were from another land.

Herod's advisors searched for knowledge and came up with the ancient prophecy of Bethlehem. Evidently, no one in Herod's court had used the stars in the quest for knowledge. They did use knowledge of the true God from the information of His prophet of old.

Herod had not always believed the Jewish rabbis and their God for he was Roman and lived in the Roman way of having many gods. He must have pondered sincerely all that he heard. If this was a child born to lead the Jewish people and create a possible future uprising against the Roman government, Herod may have felt impelled to learn more, even if having to do so meant protecting Rome by killing the newborn.

Holy Bible. King James Version. Matthew 2:7:

7 Then Herod, when he had privily called the wise men, inquired of them diligently what time the star appeared.

When Herod heard about the celestial events predicting the birth of the greatest God, he must have felt ignorant. The dignitaries before him had known years in advance to have had time to prepare for their extensive journeys. Herod could not help but wonder if what these leaders believed was true.

Each of the emissaries seeking the new Earth born God had to have been impressed when they met other important men on the same mission. It is exciting to imagine how they were taken with one another in the confirmation and reaffirmation of their beliefs in the symbolism of the movements of the stars. To meet a foreigner from another great land and find they believed as you did would have been reassuring. They were outstanding men who had never met before, meeting on enemy soil, and agreeing on all points about their immediate mission in life to represent their nations to the new God.

One can guess, when they realized Herod was an enemy, their discussions became muted with double talk and filled with intrigue as they tried to peacefully remove themselves from his court. Having seen through Herod's lies, the emissaries would ensure he'd learn from interpreters only what they wished him to hear. They would know how to say one thing and mean another while using body language to reinforce their intentions. Herod and his advisors were duped.

With the diplomacy of the present day still not perfected, can you imagine how it was back then? That Herod's insincerity was noted is not an outstanding fact. The Chinese court, for example, was learned in diplomacy and could have seen through Herod's lies instantly, for a Roman would have appeared rather crude compared to any cultured Asian courtesans.

Let's put it into another perspective. Assume *you* were the leader of a country who has just been informed that the God of all gods was going to be born on Earth. The wisest men of your kingdom, your personal counselors, astronomers and priests, told you of the events several years before they would occur. It was determined you were to visit the birth site and honor the new God.

You had much time to prepare the entourage for your journey. Excited countrymen probably maneuvered to become part of the assemblage of travelers with your entourage. The anticipation of your journey prior to the event brought excitement and wonder to your countrymen as never experienced before. Diplomatic travel to honor a new God would have perhaps been the greatest endeavor of your nation, for at no time in history had a God been born on Earth.

By the time you arrived in Judea you would have spent months journeying. It most likely came as a surprise to find the ruling authority of the province was in total ignorance of the celestial birth announcement. However, at the same time, you meet important representatives from faraway lands who not only acknowledge the identical celestial events you were following, but interpreted them as your astronomers did.

The citizens of your homeland would be anxiously awaiting your return with news of all that was experienced and witnessed. They will expect to hear all they can about the wonders of the age.

Earlier you would have had much trepidation as your priests decided what protocol to follow before this new God. Your behavior and every motion of your hands and body would have to be perfect during this greatest occasion in the existence of Earth.

You would have asked many questions. What would this God and his court expect of you? How would you enter His presence? Crawling or standing? How low should you bow? What clothing, ornaments and jewelry should be worn to illustrate the great honor and esteem you wish to extend? Will your valets dress you to be as perfect as possible to honor this God? Should you adhere to protocol currently considered correct in your land? Would the etiquette followed in your land be enough?

Everything had to be thought out with diligence for He, who will rule the heavens and the Earth, may later have opinions that would affect your homeland. Diplomatic relations will become extremely important. You would want this God to look favorably upon your country. What repercussions might there be for any mistake you made in the presence of this God? What wonder mixed with worry would *you* have felt if *you* were that ruler?

Holy Bible. King James Version. Matthew 2:8-10:

8 And he sent them to Bethlehem, and said, Go and search diligently for the young child; and when ye have found Him, bring me word again that I may come and worship Him also. 9 When they had heard the king, they departed; and, low, the star, which they saw in the east, went before them, till it came and stood over where the young child was. 10 When they saw the star, they rejoiced with exceeding great joy.

Holy Bible. King James Version. Matthew 2:11-12:

11 And when they were come into the house, they saw the young child with Mary

> His mother, and fell down, and worshipped
> Him: and when they had opened their trea-
> sures, they presented unto Him gifts; gold,
> and frankincense, and myrrh. 12 And being
> warned of God in a dream that they should
> not return to Herod, they departed into their
> own country another way.

When it was understood that Herod intended death for the new God, the emissaries must have begun preparations to keep information from this ruler. After leaving Herod, the travelers would logically have pared down their entourages, for having large caravans would have attracted attention. Unnecessary personnel would depart from your main group of travelers to return stealthily to your home land.

After seeing the magnificence of the new God, and knowing the importance of keeping Jesus safe from Herod, the emissaries would have realized Mary and Joseph could not fend off attacks from Roman soldiers. The warning to them from God required they avoid Herod reinforced their decisions. For protection, they would want to leave Herod's province quickly.

Not wanting Herod to know of their deceptions, they may have dressed like the natives to not attract attention. Traveling by night they would have lessened or avoided encounters from the locals who might later report having seen them. Herod was to have no information as to where they had been or where they were going. Trying to stealthily escape the coming wrath of Herod must have been frightful, for they had come to Bethlehem on a joyful and peaceful mission. They were not prepared for violence.

The gifts for Jesus Christ were perhaps greater in multitude than is recorded. Expecting to find the God of the universe being born into a wealthy palace court with luxuries beyond imagination, the emissaries must have been greatly humbled to find the Child resting in a lowly manger in a stable. Realizing they could not burden the brave new parents with a multitude of gifts which might become a homing beacon to King Herod and his searching minions, they knew the offerings had to be small enough to conceal and carry, yet be great enough to show homage in the correct manner. Just as gold is desired today, it was at that time in history. Gold could be easily packaged and carried on a mule, horse, or camel, and perhaps became a primary gift.

When the emissaries stealthily departed Bethlehem, Herod probably believed at least one of them would report to him before leaving the province. Herod was duped by all of these important men who slipped from his grasp.

Holy Bible. King James Version. Matthew 2:13-16:

13 And when they were departed, behold, the angel of the Lord appeareth to Joseph in a dream, saying, Arise, and take the young child and his mother, and flee into Egypt, and be thou there until I bring thee word: for Herod will seek the young child to destroy him. 14 When he arose, he took the young child and his mother by night, and departed into Egypt; 15 And was there until the death of Herod that it might be fulfilled which was spoken of the Lord by the prophet, saying, Out of Egypt have I called my Son. 16 Then Herod, when he saw that he was mocked of the wise men, was exceeding wroth, and sent forth, and slew all the children that were in Bethlehem, and in all the coasts thereof, from two years old and under, according to the

time which he had diligently inquired of the wise men.

These verses would lead us to believe that two years had passed from the time the emissaries arrived at Herod's palace to the time Herod realized the visiting dignitaries had left Judea. His anger must have been great in order for him to have committed the atrocities of slaughtering all children ages two and less. He wanted to ensure there would be no uprisings to trouble Rome. Any future king of the Jews that may cause future trouble had to be killed.

CHAPTER 2
Basic Astronomy

Basic astronomy information has been included in an easy to read format for readers over the age of ten. This was accomplished so that readers without astronomy knowledge would understand more fully the celestial birth announcements. The greatest birth announcements in the history of mankind took place during the three months prior to the birth of Jesus Christ. They culminated in the star event over Bethlehem that showed the geographical location of the royal birth. The last event was the position marker.

An important concept in astronomy is to determine where a star is located in the sky. The ways the ancient astronomers completed this task is still accomplished today by amateur astronomers. It is by use of "altitude" and "azimuth," both of which are measured in degrees.

To find how high a star is in the sky, the altitude of a star, you would use the horizon as the beginning measurement of zero-degrees ($0°$). When you are standing, the point directly above your head is called your "**zenith**" and points into space. The highest point around you is above your zenith, at 90-degrees ($90°$) altitude. When you walk around, your zenith remains above your head, unique to you. Everyone possesses their own zenith and carries it around with them.

When standing, the bottoms of your feet are in the position of your "nadir," pointing toward the center of the Earth. Your nadir also moves with you. Like your zenith, nadir is a personal possession you may not have known existed.

If you pointed your left hand at the horizon, the 0°-altitude, and your right hand at your zenith at 90°-altitude, your arms would make a right angle of 90°. Opening your arms to point from horizon to horizon would create a 180° angle, or half of a circle.

With your left arm pointing at the horizon and your right arm pointed at zenith, lower the zenith arm to the position half way between the two points. Your right arm would now be pointing above the horizon to an altitude of 45°.

The width of the little finger of your outstretched arm measures approximately 1° across the sky; the width of your hand is about 10°. Such hand measurements are currently used by amateur astronomers and students when locating stars and planets. Like the astronomers of two thousand years ago, using your fingers and hands, with careful practice you could learn to point to smaller amounts of degree changes in altitude. Point to any elevated object, whether it is a tree top or a star, and with practice you should be able to correctly determine its altitude.

The following diagram illustrates how to use your extended hands to find the altitude of objects. Remember that the horizon is 0° and the point above your head, your zenith, is at 90°.

2:1 ALTITUDE

His left hand is pointing at the 0° horizon where Earth meets the sky. His Zenith is at 90°. Halfway between his horizon and zenith is the 45° altitude position. Knowing those figures, you can determine other degrees for observations.

The horizon is where the Earth meets the sky on level ground. Once the Sun, Moon, planets, or stars are located by altitude, one has to know where they are found along the compass direction of the 360° circle around the horizon. This north-east-south-west compass direction measurement in degrees is called "azimuth".

To measure azimuth, you must be facing north. You can find north at night by knowing where the North Star is located at the end of the little dipper in the constellation, Ursa Minor. The North Star is currently located above the geographic north pole (GNP). By facing the North Star, you would be facing north.

North can also be located during the daytime by observing the direction of the noon shadow of a stick placed in the ground. The shortest shadow indicates noon and points toward north.

Whenever you face north, you are facing the 0° direction of azimuth. Your outstretched right arm would point to the east at 90° from north, your back would face south at 180° from north, and your outstretched left arm would be pointing due west at 270° from north. By practicing the degree measurements of azimuth with your arms as you did previously with altitude, you would become quite proficient at locating the compass direction of any object. Eventually you could accurately state that a star could be found so many degrees above the horizon and at a certain number of degrees from north. If anyone gave you the azimuth and altitude of a planet or star, you should be able to point right to it.

The following illustration demonstrates how to find azimuth in your own backyard.

2:2 AZIMUTH

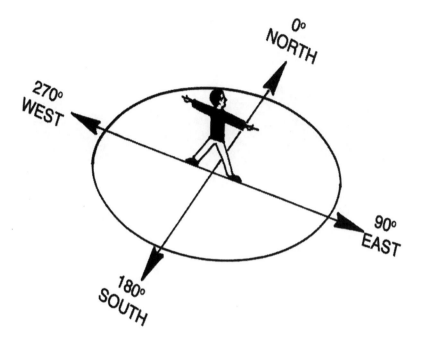

To find azimuth, locate and face north. When facing north, you are facing 0° azimuth. Your back is facing 180° azimuth (south). Your extended right hand is pointing at 90° azimuth (east) and your left hand to 270° azimuth (west). Ancient astronomers could accurately locate a star or planet position from north by using azimuth and altitude.

THE MOON

The sky that you see above the horizon includes half of the 360° orbit of the Moon, or 180°. The Moon revolves around Earth traveling about 13° toward your east each day. If you watched the evening Moon over a period of several hours, the eastward movement in front of the more stationary distant stars would be quite apparent. Actually the stars rise and set about 4-minutes earlier each day due to the Earth's **rotation** and **revolution** around the Sun. Star distances from our viewpoint are so great, they appear to not change position during our lifetime. Every star you can see is positioned in our Milky Way galaxy.

The Moon orbits the Earth in an elliptical path once per month, in approximately 27 1/3-days. Because Earth is rotating on its axis while it is revolving around the Sun, for the Moon to be directly over any site on Earth and return to that exact position in the next orbit, a wait of 29 1/3-days is necessary. The extra time is required for the Moon to make up the distance the Earth has traveled in its elliptical orbit around the Sun.

It takes the Earth one year to orbit the Sun traveling at an average speed of 107,000 kilometers per hour or 29.77 kilometers per second. Since the Earth moves 360° around the Sun in one year, the distance averages about one-degree per day.

The axis of Earth is an imaginary line running through the Earth connecting the geographic north and south poles. The Earth spins on its axis, or rotates, once in 23-hours, 56-minutes and 4.9 seconds, commonly rounded to 24-hours.

Clock time is kept by measuring the Earth's uniform rotation. The United States Naval Observatory located in Washington D.C. serves to keep the correct clock time along with the Bureau International de l'Heure in Paris, France. Measurement of the Earth spin rate is currently kept accurate by bouncing lasers off satellites and observing polar motion from observatories all over the globe. Upon occasion, the rotation of the Earth may be affected by earthquakes.

Since the rotation of the Earth is west to east, the Moon, Sun, and all celestial objects appear to rise in the east and set in the west.

Recall that the Moon is orbiting Earth. When we try to view moonrise on two consecutive days, we find on the second day the Moon has moved in its orbit toward the east and takes fifty additional minutes to rise or come into view. This was vividly pointed out to me when a friend and I were observing the Moon at moonrise two consecutive nights in a row to take pictures of Hadley Rille.

On the second night, we were busy conversing about the current celestial events as we set up the 17-inch Newtonian reflector (now owned and operated by Ohio University) and an 11-inch Celestron reflector telescope to view the Moon at the same time as the previous night. We had to wait and twiddle our thumbs for almost an hour before the Moon came into view, embarrassed to have overlooked the elementary fact of the Moon's orbit and the effect it would have on the time of our observations. We knew the facts, but in our astronomy catch up conversation, never thought about them. That was a humbling experience.

The only way you can see anything at any time is if the object is either luminous, giving off its own light, or **illuminated** by reflected light. As the Moon revolves around Earth, one half of it is always lit, or illuminated, by the Sun. We can see the surface of the Moon facing Earth only when sunlight is reflecting off it and into our eyes. The light reflecting off the Moon is called "moonshine." If we cannot see the moonshine, we cannot normally see the Moon. Due to the moon revolving around the Earth, the whole illuminated half of the moon is not always visible from Earth. That creates monthly phases, or different shapes, of the Moon.

When the Moon is directly between the Earth and Sun, during new Moon phase, the illuminated side is facing away from Earth. In that position the Moon is usually not visible from Earth. Exceptions occur when sunlight reflects off Earth (called earthshine) and hits the dark side of the Moon facing Earth. That dim light is then re-reflected, bouncing off the Moon and into our eyes.

When the Moon enters or leaves that new Moon region, between the Earth and the Sun, we see a sliver of it illuminated as the new or last crescent phase. The new crescent phase occurs right after the Moon passes between Earth and the Sun and begins to have more of the side facing Earth illuminated. At that time the lit side of the moon appears at the right side of the Moon and resembles the crescent seen on old outhouse doors. The last crescent phase occurs when the Moon has passed through all the other phases and enters once again into the region between the Sun and Earth. Viewed from Earth at that time, the illuminated crescent appears on the left side of the lunar sphere.

During the events leading up to Jesus' birth, the Moon revolved around Earth several times. When in an area to help create a significant event, it was in the new Moon stage between the Earth and the Sun. At the positions between the new and full Moon phases, we see varying amounts of the illuminated Moon depending upon where the Moon is in its orbit. Other phases of the Moon are not important in the pre-birth events and will be ignored at this time.

An **eclipse** is another term important to understand. If you brought your hand up to cover your eyes as you read this paragraph, your hand would be eclipsing the paragraph. If you closed your left eye and brought a penny towards your right eye close enough to block this paragraph, the penny would be eclipsing the paragraph. The penny is certainly much smaller than the paragraph, but due to the distance between the penny and your eye, the penny would appear to be much larger than the paragraph. The object which blocks the view or light from the further object does the eclipsing. Any obscuring of light is considered an eclipse.

The distance of celestial objects such as the Moon and Sun makes a difference in eclipses. The Sun at 1,390,000-kilometers in diameter is much larger than the Moon's 3475.9-kilometers diameter. If the Moon and Sun were side by side at the same distance, the Moon would appear no larger than a minuscule dot compared to the Sun. Due to the Moon's elliptical path, the distance between the Moon and Earth is not constant. An ellipse appears as an elongated circle or oval. It has two focus points while a circle has one. The distance between Earth and the Moon averages 384,404-kilometers. As the Moon is the closest celestial body to Earth, it can block out, or eclipse, further objects.

When the Moon passes in front of any planet, it eclipses the planet. When the Moon passes in front of the Sun it eclipses the Sun as illustrated below. An eclipse of the Sun is called a solar eclipse.

Since the Moon's path is tilted slightly from the **ecliptic**, the Moon will not be at the exact same place during its' orbit each month. As a result, when it passes between the Earth and the Sun, its position may not be in the correct alignment to create any type of eclipse.

A partial solar eclipse occurs when the Moon blocks the light from only the top or bottom portion of the Sun. When the Sun is totally eclipsed by the Moon, as in the above photograph, the hottest outer layer, the corona, becomes visible. That layer of shining white gases around the sun is normally invisible due to the brighter photosphere layer beneath it. Shaped like a crown around the Sun, changing with each second and with each eclipse, the corona resembles a glowing mass of billowing gases flowing from the Sun.

We cannot naturally see the Sun's corona until a solar eclipse occurs. The Suns' bright disk is artificially blocked at solar observatories to allow viewing of the corona for photographic images.

Due to the Moon's changing distance which alters the apparent size, the Moon does not always totally eclipse the Sun when passing in front of it. When the Moon is further from Earth during an eclipse, the outer edge of the Sun shines around the Moon to create a ring. This type of eclipse is an "annular" eclipse.

Persons who have witnessed a total solar eclipse say the experience is one they could never have imagined. The event is striking because the sky changes within minutes from full Sun to a late night condition full of stars. Eye witnesses say that when the Moon begins to cover the Sun, they can see the huge, looming shadow of the Moon approaching them in the sky. As the darkness of the Moons' shadow begins to cover their position, birds go to roost as day animals cease their activities and prepare to sleep. Night animals become active. Observers report there is an ethereal quiet, perhaps due to the confusion or fear by the animals.

Observers have also reported the event makes them feel they are participating in some religious experience. Many eye witnesses want to see another solar eclipse to experience the magnificence of the heavens and Earth and to feel the wonder of the universe working before them. I often reflect how powerful an experience a solar eclipse must have been to astronomers, priests and wisemen of 2,000-years ago who knew very little about astronomy compared that which is now known.

Just as the Moon passes in front of the Sun to eclipse it, the Sun also eclipses objects beyond it. Further planets and stars are made dim or invisible by the light of the Sun as it approaches the space in front of them.

To understand the importance the Moon had to the ancients, it is necessary to know how they perceived the Moon. To the Babylonians and their descendents, the source of all intelligence on the Earth was from the Moon god who was also the keeper of the calendar. Called "Sin" and "lord of knowledge," the Moon presided over astrological **divination**. Astrological divination means to discover what is obscure or to foretell future events sometimes by supernatural means.

The Moon god supposedly prophesied what would happen in the future by its position in the heavens and by what happened in space near it. The ancients believed constellations behind the Moon, Sun, and planets changed the interpretations and meanings of events.[1] The Babylonians compared what the Moon did with what their astronomical calendars predicted. If there were any differences, they tried to determine why. Detailed star notes such as those made by the Babylonian astronomer Naburianna were lost in time.[2] Babylonian astronomy and astrology beliefs were passed down over thousands of years. They continue to be used in the present day as the false science horoscopes found in many newspapers and magazines.

According to ancient astrologers, if the Moon god appeared in the constellation of Aries, the Moon could become an astrological candidate in the interpretation of the Christmas star. That positioning was interpreted to mean a new king would reign.

When the Moon eclipsed a planet, the ancient astronomers considered the event rare and astrologically most powerful. If the event was not visible due to clouds or weather, with their knowledge astronomers still knew the event happened. If visible, such events were considered spectacular in the dawning sky. The people of the Middle East believed the importance of any celestial event involving the Moon was magnified since the Moon was the source of all knowledge. It had been considered important through many civilizations.

Mesopotamians in 2100 B.C. called our moon "Nanna,"[3] a great lord and light shining in the sky, wearing a royal headdress.[4] In southern Iraq, a three tiered brick ziggurat monument to Nanna was built by King Ur-Nammu in honor of the moon god.[5]

Other beliefs included that when the Moon appeared to stand still, the message was for happiness. When not seen, an invasion of a major city could take place. During the time of crescent stages, when the Moon had "horns," they believed a royal prince would grow strong and the land would have good crops.

The ancient Chinese also had many symbols of associations. During the phases, they believed the Moon god **regenerated**, or was reborn. With the monthly Moon cycles of waxing (growing bigger) and waning (growing smaller), rising, setting, conjunctions, and eclipses, they assumed the Moon kept recreating itself. The Chinese believed emperors who died became the immortal gods and ascended into the sky to become a star.[6] The sacred tombs built for those held in high esteem were the points from which, they believed, the souls departed for the celestial realm.

Mondays were ruled by the Moon god. Although considered the source of intelligence, knowledge, and keeper of calendars, when seen with the Sun the interpretation was for greetings, health, and happiness while establishing the foundations of the throne of the ruler or king. When low in the sky, it meant the submission of a distant land would take place. The Moon was supposed to carry the fluidity of life, the rhythms of nature, human emotions, health, and influenced the subconscious mind.[7] The Moon god, concerned with beginnings of all areas of life, determined when you were born. Chinese called their Moon god "Yin" or "Heng." The Moon was "Luna" to others. Thus we assign the word "lunar" to an eclipse of the moon to name it a "lunar eclipse."

THE SUN

The Sun, pictured to the left, is the nearest star to Earth. At one time the Sun was considered to be one of the most important Gods. An early name of the Sun god was Sol. We live on Earth in the system of Sol, the Solar System.

The Moon rotates as it orbits Earth. Earth and the other planets rotate as they orbit the Sun. The rotating Sun is orbiting our galaxy, the Milky Way, at about 220-kilometers per second as the galaxy moves away from the Large Magellanic Cloud toward the Andromeda Galaxy. It takes about 200,000,000-years for the Sun to orbit the Milky Way once.

Stars near us are moving in the same direction and about the same speed as our Sun. Some travel less than 40-kilometers per second and others in excess of 80-kilometers per second. The Milky Way galaxy, consisting of billions of stars, carries us through the universe at a speed close to 500- kilometers per second.

Ancient men believed our Sun was the biggest and most important object in the universe. It is not. Compared to other stars, our Sun is a small, medium sized, yellow star. It is a sphere of luminous gases made of the same chemical elements which compose the Earth and other objects observed in the universe. The elements of the Sun and stars are heated to a high energy gaseous **plasma**, the fourth state of matter. The first three states of matter according to the amount of energy exhibited are solid, liquid and gas. The temperature of the photosphere, the sun's outer layer seen when you look at the sun or take a picture of it, varies between 5,500° to 6,000° Celsius. The interior of the Sun is projected to be more than 15,000,000,000° Celsius. The ancient astronomers did not realize their Sun god was a star.

Seasons are caused primarily by the tilt and parallelism of the Earth's axis. Through its' orbit, the axis of the Earth doesn't change much and remains parallel to its self with the north pole always aimed at Polaris. Polaris is also known as the Pole Star and North Star. The axis of Earth is tilted 23 1/2° from a line drawn perpendicular to the ecliptic, an extension of the Sun's equator (see illustration 2:3). As Earth orbits the Sun following the ecliptic, the parallelism of the axis tilt causes the angle of sunlight to change.

Because of the elliptical orbit, Earth is closest to the Sun in December and further away in June. The angle at which the Suns' rays hit the northern hemisphere of Earth is more vertical in June, creating warmer temperatures at that time. In December, direct rays of sunlight strike below the equator creating summer in the southern hemisphere. Winter is caused when the angle at which the Suns' rays strike the Earth is less vertical. When it is summer in the northern hemisphere, it is winter in the southern hemisphere and vise versa.

Other major planets within our solar system also orbit the Sun on the ecliptic plane. Note the position of the ecliptic plane on the following full page illustration. The ecliptic is illustrated by the dashed line extending from the Sun's equator through Earth.

To visualize the ecliptic plane, picture a DVD disk having the center hole filled with a miniature three-dimensional Sun. The flat surface of the DVD extending out from that Sun's equator in all directions represents the ecliptic.

The major planets revolve around the Sun within that ecliptic plane.[8] Since their motions follow unchanging paths, ancient astronomers could accurately predict planet positions along the ecliptic. The word planet was derived from the meaning, "wanderer," because they move through the sky along the ecliptic while true stars remain stationary. The ancient astronomers thought planets were wandering stars among stationary stars. The further from the Sun a planet is, the larger the orbit and slower the speed. The Sun also appears to move along the ecliptic path.

If you knew the position of the ecliptic in the sky, you could more correctly identify objects traveling on that path as a planet. You may locate planet positions by using current astronomical periodicals, Internet data bases, or by electronic means through computer programs designed for that purpose. Excellent mobile electronic applications, such as *Night Sky* and *SkyView*, guide users to natural and artificial celestial objects twenty-four hours a day.

2:3 AXIS TILT

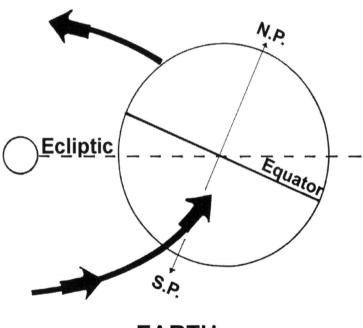

EARTH

The Earth's axis is tilted 23-1/2 degrees from a line perpendicular to the plane of Earth's orbit, also called the ecliptic. If the axis were not tilted, we would not have seasons.

By judging which stars were behind the Sun, the astronomers of ancient times foretold the seasons and annual river flooding with life-giving water, such as the rising of the Nile. Many later civilizations used the Babylonian created **zodiac** to create interpretations of celestial activity. The original zodiac was a ring of constellations dividing the ecliptic into twelve equal sections. The zodiac signs in later temples and tombs are Egyptian. Since the Greeks also lived in Egypt, the Romans considered the zodiac to be Hellenistic or Greek. The National Aeronautical & Space Administration recently added a thirteenth zodiac sign called Ophiuchus.

With their limited knowledge, the early astronomers and astrologers relied on the heavens for their wisdom. They believed the Sun god had no equal. Considered powerful and dependable, the orderly Sun was determined to be the source of *all* authority. When interpretations of events were made, if the Sun was involved, it meant there was universal approval of the event.

The Sun was used to create calendars. To many in the ancient world, the Sun created day and night, laws, social order, and was the greatest god. The round, shining Sun was understood to be a bridge between Earth, the heavens of everyday, and that which was sacred.

Modern psychologists have theorized that the circle has been a symbol which man interpreted to be a balanced whole, bringing calm and soothing the soul. This is why present day company logos or product coverings of purchased objects have circles on them, to make you feel good about them.

✵ ✵ ✵

That being the case, is it no wonder that the ancients revered circles such as the Moon and Sun? It was considered the symbol of the spirit, associated with creativity, mental concentration, self-awareness and self-expression.[9] Its shadow was used to tell time by the Mesopotamians using the "**gno-mon**," a stick placed vertically into the ground.[10] The Sun was considered to be the king of gods by the Akkadians, Asians, **Assyrians**, Babylonians, Chinese, Egyptians, Indians, Mesopotamians, and Sumerians.

Known as "An", "Any," " Ra," "Atum-Ra" and "Samas" by the Babylonians who believed it created the world and was carried by boat across the sky, it was known as "Yang" to the Chinese and "Sol" to others.[11] As the visible planets moved through their steady path along the ecliptic, the ancients could easily see Mercury, Venus, Mars, **Jupiter** and Saturn. Since the Christmas celestial events did not involve Mercury, it will not be discussed further.

2:4 ZODIAC CONSTELLATIONS

Constellation Name	Dates of Inclusion
Sagittarius	Dec 18 - Jan 18
Capricorn	Jan 19 - Feb 15
Aquarius	Feb 19 - Mar 11
Pisces	Mar 12 - Apr 18
Aries	Apr 19 – May 13
Taurus	May 14 – Jun 10
Gemini	Jun 20 – Jul 20
Cancer	Jul 21 – Aug 9
Leo	Aug 10 – Sep 15
Virgo	Sep 16 – Oct 30
Libra	Oct – 31 Nov 22
Scorpio	Nov 23 – Nov 29
Ophiuchus	Nov 30 – Dec 17

VENUS

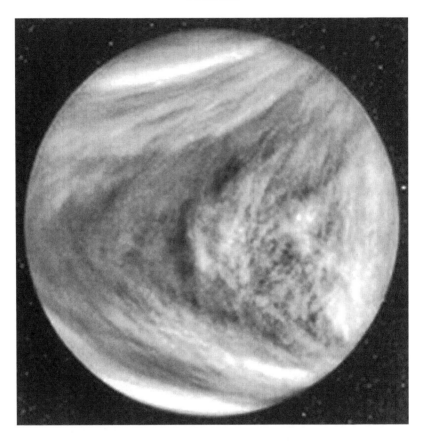

Venus is the closest planet to Earth. Since Venus' surface is covered with highly reflective clouds, it has what is called a high **albedo**. Albedo refers to the percent of reflected light. Venus reflects about ninety percent of all sunlight to become the third brightest object in our sky, the Sun being first and the Moon second in brightness. Due to the brilliance, Venus was considered to be very important.

The red star **Sirius** was recorded to be the fourth brightest object in the sky before Christ's birth. When you observe the constellation of Orion, Sirius is the brilliant star located to the lower left of the constellation. Sirius has since that time evolved into a blue star much more quickly than present day astronomers have predicted a star to change temperature and color.

Venus may have been symbolized as an eight-pointed star because it repeats the same evening-morning star pattern every eight years. The eight-pointed figure appeared on many coins minted in the Roman city of Antioch. There has been controversy over the eight-pointed star symbol and the importance attributed to it.[14]

To some archaeologists, the eight-pointed star represents only an Antioch mint mark to show the origin of the coins. To others, it signifies an important celestial event. That coins minted in Antioch with symbols of the Moon, planets and stars can be used to show the importance celestial events had on the populace.

Ancient Babylonians originated the Venus names "Ishtar," and "Bilbat." [15] The Egyptians symbolized the planet as the "Bennue", a heron-like bird commonly equated with the phoenix, a bird that dies and comes back to life. That may have been due to Venus moving behind the Sun, periodically disappearing from view, and reappearing later. They thought Venus had been reincarnated or reborn.

The Venus god supposedly gave birth to Romulus and Remus who founded Rome. Considering Venus extremely important, the Babylonians left tablets with over seven thousand astrological interpretations involving the planet. [16]

Any event occurring when Venus was visible in the dawn sky was interpreted to affect royalty, nations, agriculture, health, and the outcome of wars. Believed to be the god that started the astrological forecasts of the future, Venus is the god of love, beauty, and harmony and rules the constellation of Taurus. The Babylonians believed the god brought sympathy and pleasure.[17] The Sumerians considered her the queen of heaven.

2:5 SIRIUS

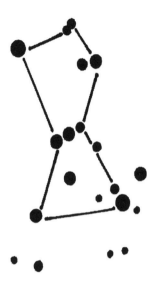

As illustrated, the brightest star Sirius is seasonally located to the lower left of the constellation Orion. They appear in the night sky in the northern hemisphere. Orion is usually recognized as a large rectangle with the three angled stars across the center. The upper left star of Orion is the red star Betelgeuse.

MARS

Since Mars is further from the Sun than Earth with a larger orbital path, the planet takes longer to orbit the Sun. Because Earth moves faster within its smaller orbit, Earth overtakes Mars and passes it at least once a year. The ancient astronomers could not figure out what was happening in the sky when Earth overtook and passed Mars, for as Earth whizzed by in its speedy orbit, Mars would appear to move backwards, or display what is called "**retrograde**" motion.

Retrograde motion can be explained by observing a very common occurrence on Earth, such as when your car passes another on the highway. If you were in the faster, passing car, you would see the slower car traveling in the same direction as yourself as you approached. When you were actually passing the slower car, the slower vehicle would appear for a short time to move backwards. As you move further on the highway beyond the slower vehicle, you would observe again that both cars would appear to be moving in a forward motion.

This is the same effect observed when Earth approaches and passes Mars. The planet can be seen moving forward, but as Earth passes it, Mars appears to move backwards for a short time. This is the retrograde motion that perplexed ancient astronomers.

Due to its red color, Mars was thought to be covered with blood and considered to be the god of war.[18] As such, it was associated with the horrors of combat. The more important the military was to a country, the more important Mars became as the war god. Mars was also viewed as an agricultural god that protected the harvest against disease and bad weather.

Mars ruled over Judea. Any astronomical event of Mars connected with Judea was to be considered positive, especially if Mars appeared in front of the constellation Aries. Aries was important as that constellation also represented Judea. The two together doubled the meaning. Inversely, any celestial event considered to be important to Judea had to involve Mars to increase the strength of the interpretations.

Mars was involved in celestial events which preceded the birth of Jesus Christ as part of the heavenly birth announcement. The presence of the planet intensified astrological implications and gave more magnificence to the birth of the new God. When Mars appeared to the left of the Moon, it meant the king would act with might. When Mars met the Moon in a conjunction, the interpretation was that the king will grow powerful and have no rival. When near Venus, it meant that victory was near. Mars was known to be practical rather than hold ideals.[19] The presence of Mars at any birth produced leaders and sportsmen who were supposed to have sharp perceptions and make incisive decisions. The new God was to be one with will power who would assert himself when needed.[20]

Mars was known as "Ares" in Greece, "Mars" in Rome, "Nergal" and "Mustabarru-mutany" in Babylonia, and "Horus" in Egypt.

JUPITER

Jupiter was an important celestial god to the ancient astronomers because it was the largest "wanderer" crossing the heavens. After the Sun and Moon, Jupiter was considered the god of gods and protector of Earth. Because the great size and resulting gravitational attractions to objects in space, the positioning of Jupiter protects our world in real life. Objects that might strike Earth are pulled into Jupiter instead.

In Babylon, the Jupiter god was believed to be the creator of the world and natural laws, the king of kings and a fortunate omen in the sky.[21] The planet created order, an event celebrated by Babylonians in the spring or fall. To the Romans, Jupiter was the king who went on to father Mars and who, like his father, had affairs with Venus.

Jupiter was the ruler of Wednesday and considered a good omen when in the sky. Seen during a solar eclipse meant there would be peace. The planet was the principal god relating to protecting the rights of humans.[22] It ruled the councils of the other gods with wisdom, benevolence, and justice, showing compassion when needed. Considered generous, truthful, cheerful and friendly, Jupiter was believed to be a philosopher who made long journeys. The Assyrians believed if Jupiter was near or involved in an eclipse, the king involved would have peace and his name would be honored.

In 7 A.D. Jupiter and Mercury joined in a conjunction, or appeared to meet. To the people of that time, Jupiter was the symbol of dominance and power while Mercury symbolized property, national treaties and negotiations. The conjunction was marked on a coin minted in Antioch shortly after the occurrence. I mention this incident to illustrate that such an event, occurring years after Jesus' birth, was still considered so important that it was placed on a coin.

SATURN

Second only to Jupiter in size after the Sun and Moon, and an important celestial object, the Saturn god was given the designation as the king of gods until later disposed of by Jupiter.

To the Greeks and Romans, Saturn was the father of the Olympian gods and the god of agriculture, associated with the planting and sowing of seed and harvest, a fertility god. The name Saturn may have been derived from "sator", an early word meaning "sower of seed." Ancient astronomers believed the harvest was due to the god Saturn. Saturn was celebrated with a week-long party during December 17-24 called Saturnalia. It was during this celebration that the pardoning of some criminals took place by the Romans.[23]

Saturnalia was replaced by a December celebration recognizing the birth time of Jesus Christ. It was believed to be a logical move when Emperor Aurelian of Rome became a Christian. He believed the citizens of the Roman world would not give up their riotous holiday of Saturnalia and designated that holiday as the time of Jesus' birth. He assumed if the people retained a purpose for that holiday, they would more easily convert to Christianity. Because of this, the birth of Jesus Christ became an event celebrated in late December.

December 25th is not the true date of Jesus' birth. The original date of Jesus' birth had been lost in history and not found until now.

To the Babylonians and their descendents, Saturn was like the Sun god and considered the bull of the heaven. Ruling Saturday, Saturn was the protector of the Jewish people, the youngest Titan, and father of the Olympian gods. Practical and wise, this god was linked with politics and friendships. To have been born when Saturn was present in the sky with Jupiter, the interpretation was that the child would become a genius and create a steadying influence.

The Babylonians originated the planet names for Saturn such as "Ninib", "Niurta" or "Kaimann." It was known As "Kronos" in Greece, "Saturn" in Rome, and "Horus" (this Horus has a falcon head topped with bull horns) in Egypt.

CHAPTER 3
Ancient Symbolism

ASIANS

Could an Asian emissary been one of the wisemen? The early people inhabiting the Soviet Caucasus, the "Ossetes," used a well designed calendar with the dawn relationships explained using maps. As with the Chinese, the directions that celestial objects moved took on special meanings.

The shaman-like, religious priests acknowledged their main god lived in the sky. For persons residing from the Soviet Caucasus up through Siberia, the Sun was considered the source of all law, social order, and authority. Since they made predictions of the celestial events, they could have foretold the birth of Jesus Christ and sent an emissary to Bethlehem.

BABYLONIANS

The Babylonians are important as later civilizations used their beliefs and data to create their own astronomy legends and understanding. Iraq is the present day region of ancient Babylon. People inhabiting that region were mathematically advanced and used the stars to determine the fate of nations. The studies of the stars, cosmology, and astronomy of the movements in the heavens were applied to the destinies of all royal persons and the lands they inhabited. They are important because their symbolism, interpretations and beliefs were followed by astronomers of later time periods.

Babylonians believed "**Shamash**," the Sun god, witnessed and judged everything representing celestial objects. Within a hundred years of Jesus' birth, the astronomers created calendars and scheduled events and ceremonies up to a year or more in advance. They believed they knew the order of the **cosmos** was given them by the gods with whom they were in communication.

The Babylonians inscribed their astronomical observations on clay tablets as early as 3,000 years before the birth of Jesus as they recorded and accurately predicted the movements of the visible planets, lunar cycles, and eclipses. It is from their observations they originated their science of astrological readings, known today as horoscopes. It is believed that the rulers used such forecasts to protect their lands from invaders.

The Babylonians made the different groups of stars into constellations, creating mythical figures of gods for each. They decided planets moving through these constellations foretold astrological events taking place in the future. There are currently eighty-eight recognized constellations.

CHINESE
Could one of the wisemen at the birth of Christ been Chinese? Why not? They too were an ancient country with priests who believed very strongly in the symbolism of the heavens, who could predict celestial happenings, and would know what was going to transpire. They also used the stars to predict future events and thought of the observable sky as a living, spiritual being. They believed the stars foretold all events, including births, love, and wars. Using only dawn observations, the priests foretold the future using symbols to create their interpretations and meanings. In

addition, they would have traveled from the east to arrive at Bethlehem.

The event which precipitated the Chinese love of astronomy occurred when five planets lined up like a string of pearls near the constellation Pegasus on the day of the spring **equinox**, February 26, 1953 B.C. The Chinese began a national astronomical calendar from that event.

The Chinese emperor participated in ceremonies to help the cosmos continue. In his sacred role, he played the part of an intermediary between heaven and Earth, coordinating anything between the gods of heaven and Earthlings. Qin shi Huang di, who died in 221 B.C., was placed in a tomb which was astronomically oriented with the primary compass directions of north, east, south, and west.

Since it was the emperor's business to assist in all celestial happenings, he would most likely want to pay homage to and honor the new God. That a representative from their nation, if not the emperor himself, journeyed from China west to Bethlehem as one of the kings to acknowledge the birth of Jesus Christ would be viewed as logical.

What would the Chinese offer the new God? Perhaps incense, as it was commonly used during celestial ceremonies, considered very important, and was valuable.

We know ships sailed through most of Earth's waters for mapmakers as far back as 13,000 years ago left drawings showing the ocean and land world as they knew it. Phoenicians sailors, known to have navigated and sailed their ships throughout the oceans, could have brought the Chinese partway to Bethlehem.

During Roman times the eastern ocean trade routes included those through the Red Sea, the Persian Gulf, the Arabian Sea, the Bay of Bengal, eastward toward the Mekong Delta, and further north along the coastal routes. It is highly likely the Chinese emperor with his entourage of support staff was brought by ship to the southeastern region of the Arabian Peninsula or Persian Gulf, before being dropped off to make the rest of the journey to Bethlehem by horse or camel.

In addition to the Phoenicians, Tarshish ships sailed from what is now the peninsula of southern Spain. Phoenician and Tarshish ships transported passengers and goods throughout their known world.

Astronomers were important in China. They were given honor, wealth, palaces, and many wives. They were so wealthy they could have been mistaken for a king when meeting Herod. Such astronomers have not been so honored or wealthy since that time in history. However, no matter how honored or wealthy they were, if one of their predictions was wrong, they were beheaded.

EGYPTIANS

The Egyptians had been important in astrology, astronomy, and cosmology of the ancient civilizations. They also used dawn observations in their daily worship and study of their heavenly gods. The Persians and other civilizations learned from the Egyptians about the cosmological events and followed in their footsteps. Many of the Egyptian temple rituals were copied by the Persian, African, and Asians. This is important to remember as it may have been a Persian, African, or Asian who was one of the wisemen to visit the Christ child in Bethlehem.

The Egyptians named the Sun "Amun-Red", "Re", and "Ra", the ruler of the daylight hours. The importance Egyptians gave their Sun god is noted by their placing the main axis of the Great Temple of Amun-Red at Karnack, Egypt pointing to the summer **solstice** Sun. Another temple to the southeast had the axis aligned with the winter solstice sunrise.[3] Not all temples were built to line up with the Sun, but perhaps with other celestial objects which are no longer in those positions due to Earth's **precession**.

The imaginary axis is a line drawn between the geographic north and south poles and around which the Earth rotates. As the Earth's rotation slows, the axis wobbles much like that of a slowing, spinning top. This wobble is called precession. As precession moves the earth's position, stars that lined up previously with monuments and temples built thousands of years ago will be off center in this century.

The ancient positioning of the northern star field can be determined by present day computer programs discussed later in this investigation. As current astronomers have found, nothing in the universe is stationary. All stars in our galaxy are moving in different directions and at varying speeds away from us. None appear to be in the same position as they were when the great temples of ancient Egypt were constructed.[4] Their north-south alignment is only off by 1/12th of a degree which may be due to the precession of earth's axis.[5]

Right now the north geographic pole is pointing to the star Polaris. Polaris is also known as the North Star located in the constellation of Ursa Minor, the little bear. As the precession of the axis continues, the north pole will eventually point elsewhere.

One full precessional wobble of Earth takes about 25,000 years. That means in 25,000-years the Earth will have created one whole wobble and be back to the same position as it is today. Since all objects in the universe are moving, Polaris will no longer be above the current north pole. It will have moved to another location.

Illustration 3:1 shows how the Earth will move from the current position. The north and South Poles will precess to a position forty-seven degrees away.

It is possible the great pyramid which Cheops built may have been for astronomical reasons before it was sealed, for the south face was aimed at the noon Sun on the day of winter solstice, perhaps to reflect the sunlight back to the origin god.

Egyptian carvings and paintings illustrate purification ceremonies completed prior to the dawn Sun god offerings. The heavens were mapped and that knowledge placed on temple pillars.[6] **Pharaohs** were considered the god-kings. In the morning rite, the reigning Pharaoh would stand before a statue of the Sun god, open the statue, and prostrate himself before it. The cloth robe which covered the god statue would be changed, much like the present day seasonal changing of the vestments in the Christian churches and sashes of Buddhist statues.

The Pharaoh made motions as though feeding the statue, colored the face of the statue, and placed upon it royal insignia. This daily morning ritual took place over many years by many Pharaohs. It's possible the statue was so treated because they could not touch the actual Sun god which brought life to the world.

French Egyptologists have studied other carved relief inscriptions and found astronomical references to the rising Sun in the chapel to the rear of Amun-Red and in the Festival Hall proper. There is a lower room which has an inscription inviting persons to watch the sunrise. The Egyptian inscriptions highlight the importance of the dawn observations and the rising Sun. One inscription refers to visitors who walk toward the viewing hall to see the horizon, or climb to the lonesome place of the soul, to the high room of the ram who sails. That may refer to the Zodiac sign of Aries, the mythical ram which appears in the March sky when the Sun passes the equinox and begins to rise in the sky.

Aries is considered the first sign of the Zodiac which the Sun enters. On the day of the Spring Equinox direct rays of sunlight strike the equator, an imaginary line equidistant between the north and south poles. The equinox is always a day of exactly 12-hours of daylight and 12-hours of darkness at every location on Earth. "Equi" means "equal" and "-nox" means "night".

The spring equinox would have been an auspicious time. It marked the day when the length of the daylight hours began to increase until the longest day of the year was reached, the summer solstice.

3:1 PRECESSION

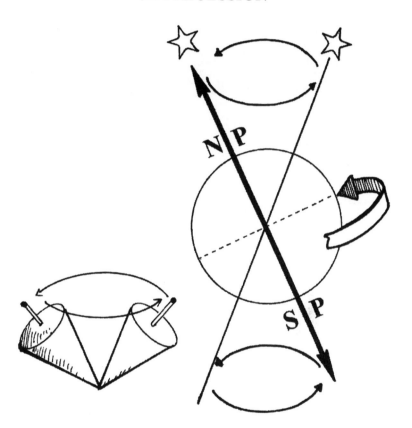

This diagram illustrates how the northern and southern geographic poles will precess in a circle as the Earth rotation slows. Earth wobbles much like a slowing top. One full precession takes a little over 25,000-years. Polaris is the current star above the north pole. The north star 5,000 years ago was Thuban. The star Vega will be over the north pole in 14,000 A.D.

The summer solstice marked the day when the daylight hours began to decrease. About September 22nd, when the autumnal equinox occurred, the Sun was over the Earth's equator. After the autumnal equinox, the daylight hours in the northern hemisphere grew progressively shorter until the winter solstice, when the Sun was furthest south at dawn.

The Egyptian god "Ra" was the ruler of each day and giver of all that existed, including the life-giving Nile River. The hieroglyph of the Sun during that time period was identical to the word "king". When the Sun rose at dawn, the ancient Egyptians believed the land was renewed. The Egyptians, like the Chinese, believed that upon death their pharaoh would ascend into the sky to become a star.

There is one theory, gleaned from the Egyptian pyramids, that when the pharaohs ascended to the sky after their earthly death, the pyramid was the stepping stone to the stars, a sacred place which connected the Earth to the heavens. The souls, it was believed, rose at sunrise and returned to their tombs at nights. The rising Sun, such as that symbolized on a falcon ornament worn on the kilt of Tutankhamen, identified the royal family and wearer as related to the Sun.

Designs on buildings symbolized the original creation of Earth and the purposes of the heavens. In Egypt, an area rich in symbolic expressions of art, architecture and life, the significance of the Sun was important. In relief art on the walls of the buildings, the flesh of some gods was depicted in yellows and gold for the day Sun and in red for the rising and setting Sun.

Ra ruled the forces of the Nile and all life. The hieroglyph of the word Sun/king was the Sun rising from a mound of creation. In the daily reestablishment of world order as the Sun rose, the Pharaoh was reenergized as the Earth was renewed. The rising Sun was considered the rebirth of a dead Pharaoh. There are carvings in the walls of one stone chamber describing how a Pharaoh ascended into the sky and regulated the night, sending hours on their way. Other Egyptian tombs are filled with astronomical images of the Sun which confirm the link between life, death, and the objects in the sky.

The predawn reappearances of the "**decans**," the stars which brought the dawn, were symbolized to be the rebirth of different gods. They would reappear in the sky after an absence recognized as the death of the god. Not knowing the Earth revolved around the Sun, the ancient astronomers assumed the coming and going of the stars and planets were due to the death and rebirth of the gods whom the objects represented.

The sky was an eternal constant. It provided images which gave the concept of immortality of life after death. It was always there while mortal life on Earth would come and go.

The Egyptian culture existed for many years, the symbolism of celestial events staying with the same meanings. The leading pharaohs for the 100-years before the birth of Jesus Christ were members of the Ptolemy family, a time when there was much influence by Greek rulers and travelers. The many gods being worshipped by the Greeks influenced the Egyptian religion, while Greek life styles influenced Egyptians life styles, especially with art and literature. The Egyptians came to be regarded as lower class citizens and were eventually downgraded socially to almost nothing.

The Ptolemy families tried to bring the Greek empire into Egypt, the last Ptolemy ruler being Cleopatra's son by Caesar, Ptolemy XVI. That forced influence stopped when Egypt was declared a Roman province after the death of Cleopatra. The Romans occupied Egypt for less than 100-years prior to the birth of Jesus Christ. Even though the country was overcome by the Romans, there remained within it a pocket of intelligence which retained the old methods, old beliefs, secret meetings, hidden religions and other things anti-Greece and Anti-Rome. The priests probably taught descendents about the importance of their Egyptian gods and astronomy.

MESOPOTAMIANS: AKKADIANS & ASSYRIANS

The Mesopotamians, Akkadians, Sumerians, Assyrians, Babylonians, Egyptians, Persians, Chinese, Asians, and Indians all used the Sun as their primary god. The Mesopotamians believed the existence of men was only to serve their gods.[7] Their beliefs influenced future generations setting the importance of studying movements of heavenly bodies.

From 2360-2180 B.C., during the Akkadian period of Mesopotamia, official stamps made by rolling a small fired clay cylinder with three dimensional markings into soft clay have been found. The impression they made would be used like that of a signet ring to make an identifying mark in an official wax seal. In the British Museum, one cylinder stamp portrays the Sun god, "Shamash," which emits rays of waving light as he rises between two mountains.[8] The goddess Venus, or "Ishtar," positioned as the morning star on the left, witnessed the appearance of the Sun. Whenever the Moon, Sun, and Venus appeared together on a stamp, they became a celestial stamp of approval for anything, just as the planet gods approved of objects when they were in the sky. They occupied the role as creators and sustainers of order of Mesopotamia when they assumed the characteristics of Jupiter, called "Marduk." The Mesopotamian celestial observations were so accurate, they were later used by historians to determine the years the kings reigned.[9]

The Marduk temple complex, home of the tower of Babel which stood for their link between the heavens and the Earth, was the largest of all Babylonian temples. The gods which it contained had tiaras made of gold and the deep blue, semi-precious gem, lapis lazuli. There are numerous writings describing the buildings having roofs covered with gold leaf shining in the Sun, much like the current Buddhist temples of Southeast Asia. The gold leaf covering the bronze inlay on the doors of cedar wood paneling and pillars was one of the many riches mentioned in historical writings.

The Assyrian period of Mesopotamia also had a stamp exhibiting the Sun, Moon and Venus. To the Assyrians, the Sun was considered the creator and sustainer of order and the Moon a great god. The heavens were studied and predictions made from what they could measure. If the celestial events did not unfold as the priests predicted, they were concerned. Any error on the part of the priests would lead to a reevaluation of their studies and perhaps new symbolic interpretations. By 800 B.C. the Assyrians believed most everything was predicted and controlled by celestial events.[10]

PERSIANS

Scholars believe one of the wisemen to visit the Christ child in Bethlehem originated in Persia because Persian astronomers consistently searched the sky for omens of three **Zoroastrian** messiahs. The Zoroastrian religion was founded in Persia by Zoroaster.

His followers had been waiting and searching for over 500-years to find precursors to their three predicted messiahs, finally giving up astronomy for astrology. They had believed there was one eternal god of the universe who was going to send three messiahs to mankind on Earth. When they interpreted the signs of Jesus' birth they may have assumed it was their first messiah being born. They would have brought their caravans and gifts to the new god, becoming one of the caravans of Magi.

The Persians, in what is now Iran, were influenced by the Egyptian religions and Sun worship. Ptolemy began his Alexandrian calendar from Persian observations, illustrating the importance of Persian techniques adopted by the Greeks. When the Greeks overcame Egypt, many Egyptians moved into Persia taking with them their manner of dress, knowledge, religious traditions and customs.

SUMERIANS

The greatest Sumerian god, "An" or "Any", had a symbol identical with the word "diugir" also meaning shining or Sun-like. The Sumerians held the Sun to be the most important god. Any celestial action of importance had to involve the Sun.

The **Sumer** civilization was one of the oldest in southern Mesopotamia. They believed every natural force was a god while man was but a slave to the many gods.[11] Their beliefs influenced future religions.

CHAPTER 4
Christmas Star Events

A stronomers have assumed the famous Christmas star event occurred at night and searched within their computer programs for an event which would match their criteria. They were wrong. As mentioned earlier, the time for celestial observations of the heavenly gods by astronomers and astrologers at that time in history was primarily during the predawn hours.

An early example of dawn observations can be made by investigating the prehistoric **megalith**s, or monuments, found throughout Europe, Africa, Ethiopia, Sudan, Palestine, Iran, Pakistan, Tibet, India, Southeast Asia, Japan, Borneo, and around the Mediterranean. Used for observations of special events, especially solstices and equinoxes, the sighting lines used on the megaliths function primarily for dawn observations.

At the time of Christ, all of the dots of light seen in the dark sky were called stars. No one knew there were planets traveling within the star fields. As previously mentioned, astronomers thought they were "wandering stars."

To illustrate, if you went outside and looked up at a clear sky tonight, could you tell which were stars and which were planets? Unless you had studied astronomy, the answer would most likely be no, even though you attended school and would be considered educated. The majority of persons who lived at the time of Jesus Christ had no education and knew nothing about astronomy. They also referred to any point of light in the sky as a star.

Most planets we can see without a telescope appear much larger than the background stars. The author took this 2012

photograph of the planets Jupiter and Venus at opposition to illustrate the difference in size.

In the past, astronomers searching for an evening Christmas star event often covered a fifteen year range, going back into the B.C. (Before Christ) years. I began my research using this multi-year time frame. The hour of the events for which I searched had to occur at dawn within the Bethlehem time zone. I discovered not just one solitary event, but a progression of birth announcements occurring that culminated in a spectacular event over Bethlehem in Judea.

If you were in Bethlehem at the time of Christ's birth, you could have looked straight up into the sky at dawn to see the last event happening. What occurred, as verified by several astronomy computer programs, took place in the twilight hours of dawn over a period of several months when the ancient astronomers viewed their celestial gods to interpret the messages, request alms, gifts, sustenance, healthy crops, and obtain healing.

Using their mathematics and knowledge of the motions of the Sun, Moon and what they called wandering stars, the astronomers of that time used symbolism to predict what would happen in the future. Several spectacular celestial occurrences foretold the birth of this new omnipotent God.

It was for these predicted dawn events that emissaries prepared for their journeys, planning their sailing and/or overland travel to Bethlehem far enough in advance to allow for the assembly of their supporting entourages, creation and organization of the presentation gifts, and adequate travel time. Beginning preparations a year or more in advance, they may have been traveling with their caravans many months before reaching Herod's palace.

The following events list the celestial phenomena which created the most magnificent birth announcement of all time for the birth of Jesus Christ.

Some titles by which He was known were: Anointed of the Lord, Christ, Christ the Lord, Counselor, Everlasting Father, Foundation of Salvation, Immanuel, Holy One of Israel, Lamb of God, Lord God, Lord, Messiah, Mighty God, Prince of Peace, Savior, Son of David, Son of God, Son of the Highest, Son of Joseph, and Wonderful.

His names included: Iesous & Jesus (Greek), Iesus & Jesu (Latin), Jahshua (India), Jehoshua & Yeshua (Hebrew), Jeshua (Dead Sea Scrolls), Jesus (English), Yeshu (Sanskrit & Arabic), Yeshua & Joshua (Semitic), Yuz Asaf (Northwest India), and Yuza (Persian).

EVENTS IN THE CELESTIAL BIRTH ANNOUNCEMENTS OF JESUS CHRIST

EVENT # 1: JULY 1, 0004 A.D.

__FACT__: The Moon and Jupiter made their appearance in the sky together as the Sun rose. If the astronomers had had telescopes, they would have also seen the dwarf planet Pluto and the planet Neptune just north of the Moon while the planet Uranus was to the southeast. The rising Sun was in the sky by Venus, Mars and the Moon.

It is common to see either Mercury or Venus by the Sun, but not Mars and Venus and the Moon so close together. Venus, Mars, and Jupiter were at opposition, meaning were positioned in their orbital path beyond the Sun. Their full faces were illuminated and extremely brilliant in the morning sky.

__ANCIENT SYMBOLIC INTERPRETATION:__ The presence of the Sun god and Moon god together forecast greetings, happiness, good health, and established a foundation for the throne of the ruler in power. The unusual brilliance of all the planets in opposition at the same time illustrated how the gods were asking astronomers to pay attention for what was to come, like numerous neon signs in the sky.

FACT: When the Sun rose for an hour to an altitude position of fifteen-degrees above the horizon, it was within a few degrees of Venus. Because of its dense cloud cover, Venus reflects over ninety percent of the sunlight which hits it. Being at opposition and in full phase it was exceptionally bright. Mars and the Moon were about one degree apart and about ten degrees east of the Sun. In elevation, they were halfway between the horizon and zenith. Although in the new moon phase and not visible, the astronomers were aware of its presence and knew exactly where it was. The Moon and Mars were within 15-degrees of the constellation of kings, Leo the Lion.

ANCIENT SYMBOLIC INTERPRETATION: The July 1st event is equated with Venus, the goddess of fertility, foretelling a birth. At any birth, the ancient astronomers believed what the god stars in the sky represented would be true for any child being born at that time. Since Venus was also the god of love, modern Christians might assume Venus was chosen to become part of the birth announcement of the God who requested everyone love one another.

Venus represented a rebirth and was associated with the Phoenix, a bird that dies and comes back to life. That the new God would rise from the state of death would also have been expected. An additional interpretation of the god star Venus was that it affected royalty, nations and the outcome of wars. The child being born would therefore become royal, cause changes in nations, and the outcome of wars.

Mars was the war god, protector of the country, the god of the growing harvest who fought against plant disease, the guardian of good weather, and protector of Judea. When in the sky, Mars magnified for Judea all that transpired, including the importance of any god being born.

When the Mars god and Venus god were near one another, the symbolism meant victory would prevail. This was interpreted to mean that nothing could stop the coming birth of the new God. The presence of Mars, with reference to a birth, was supposed to produce a leader who would have sharp perceptions. The new God would understand what he saw and make incisive decisions by going straight to the heart of a matter to penetrate through layers of deception before making conclusions or judgments. In other words, he would know all. The presence of Mars forecast a God with will power who would assert Himself when needed.

Mars, Venus and Saturn were all at opposition and extremely brilliant.

EVENT #2: AUGUST 25, 0004 A.D.

FACT: Mars rose three hours before the Sun. Venus rose an hour before the Sun. Saturn rose in the sky after Venus. The moon was entering crescent phase. The Sun, with three brilliant shining planets above it in the dawning sky, caught up with the unblemished Saturn and moved in front of it, eclipsing the planet. Saturn remained eclipsed by the Sun for four days. Eclipses have always been a major event for astronomers. This was the most spectacular episode in this series of events so far.

ANCIENT SYMBOLIC INTERPRETATION: The eclipse of the Saturn god was interpreted to mean that the Sun god, worshipped as the giver of life, eclipsed the ruler of the universe and father of all kings, Saturn. By being eclipsed, the Saturn god was shown to have lost some significance and became subordinate to the coming new God of the universe and of all creation. Saturn and the Sun joined in agreement as rulers and givers of life to celebrate the birth of the new God. The ancient astronomers would therefore interpret this to mean the Sun and Saturn agreed that the new God was to live and rule. The Venus god and Mars god were present to bear witness and join in agreement.

EVENT #3: AUGUST 30, 0004 A.D.

FACT: When the Sun rose in the morning sky, the extremely bright Saturn became visible as the Sun moved slowly from in front of the ringed planet. The eclipse of Saturn was ending.

ANCIENT SYMBOLIC INTERPRETATION: The Saturn god was one of the rulers of the universe and father of all kings, the ruler of the abundant harvest, and a giver of life. To have such a deity present was an ominous sign of greatness in the celestial sphere, for it influenced the rest of the wandering stars and brought them greatness. Anything that happened in the sky in the presence of Saturn was thought to be magnified in importance.

FACT: There were five brilliant objects lined up in the sky at the prime time of astronomical observations, the dawn of a new day. They were: Mars, the Moon, Venus, the Sun and Saturn. During its orbit, Saturn moved westward toward the position where it would eventually pinpoint Bethlehem. Mars and Venus rose higher in the morning sky.

ANCIENT SYMBOLIC INTERPRETATION: The Mars god and Venus god moved higher to show the rise of their importance. Anything of significance that would happen in Judea must have the presence of Mars, the Judean protector and God. Saturn appeared in the morning sky still moving from behind the Sun god to show that it was subordinate to the new God of the universe and of all creation. After the eclipse, it had remained for several days behind the Sun god to show the subordination would last. When the Sun god moved past Saturn, that god would be seen to still shine in brilliance, proving it would again grow in power to rule what was needed. Ancient astronomers would agree that Saturn and the Sun had joined in agreement to become a mighty celestial force.

FACT: The Moon, in crescent phase and close to the sun, appeared above Venus.

ANCIENT SYMBOLIC INTERPRETATION: Positioned close to one another, the Moon god and Venus god watched the king of gods, Saturn, continue to emerge from the eclipse. For all three gods to be in the same location in the sky was of great significance to astronomers. Once again, the celestial occurrences meant the heavenly gods were trying to announce a great happening on the Earth: the birth of the mightiest God to ever exist.

EVENT #4: AUGUST 31, 0004 A.D.

FACT: The fourth significant event in Jesus' birth announcement happened the very next day. At sunrise, the planets remained at opposition and at their most brilliant. The upper sky containing Mars was still dark before the Sun's light reached it. As Venus rose above the horizon, the Moon moved in front of Venus and partially eclipsed it. Saturn was still emerging from being eclipsed by the Sun. Therefore, there were two partial eclipses visible at the same time.

<u>ANCIENT SYMBOLIC INTERPRETATION</u>: The Venus god was partially eclipsed by the god of knowledge, the Moon. Therefore, the Venus god was shown to be not as powerful as before, for its might had been overshadowed, or eclipsed, by the all knowing Moon god. That any eclipse occurred was noteworthy. To have two happen at once was outstanding. Remember, on August 25th, the Saturn god was eclipsed. On August 31, Venus was partially eclipsed. These two major events happened within a few days. But one day after Venus was partially eclipsed; another even more major event took place.

Significant events were occurring rapidly, one right after another. Astronomers all over Earth probably had difficulty believing what they saw as the majesty of the heavens kept them anticipating events they had previously forecast. What a wonder it must have been to those ancient astronomers to forecast these events, anticipate them, and then watch them unfold before their eyes. If one major happening was ominous, here were one after another after another. The significance could not have been lost on the people of their generation.

EVENT #5: SEPTEMBER 1, 0004 A.D.

<u>FACT</u>: The fifth significant event of Jesus' birth announcement occurred on September 1st, 0004 when a spectacular solar eclipse occurred close to Mars, Venus, and Saturn while the Sun was partially eclipsing the slow moving Saturn. Venus, Mars and Saturn were still at opposition and brilliant. The Moon then moved in front of the Sun and totally eclipsed it. To have the Sun eclipsing Saturn and the Moon eclipsing the Sun simultaneously is an extremely rare event at any time, let alone for a dawn sky. It did not matter that the Sun's brilliance blocked out Saturn for the astronomers knew where Saturn was. As the Moon blackened the Sun and blocked the sunlight, Saturn's image would have brightened to allow it to appear like a jewel of light beaconing for attention in the sky.

During our lifetime, solar eclipses have occurred primarily near noon. There is a written record of a solar eclipse at sunrise found in the British Museum on a Babylonian record from 15 April, 136 B.C. documenting a solar eclipse occurring ninety-six minutes after sunrise.[1] The changing positions of the Earth during precession of the axis and the fact that the orbit of the Moon is not on the ecliptic plane have perhaps changed the time frame of solar eclipses over the last several thousand years.

ANCIENT SYMBOLIC INTERPRETATION: The great Sun god was shown to bow down and become subordinate to the coming God of all creation. This was accomplished by the Moon, god of all knowledge, moving in front of and hiding from view the strong and important Sun god. So far, three great gods had been bowed before the predicted new God. Mars, the protector god, watched over all to ensure nothing would interfere. By his presence, the war god Mars magnified the importance Judea would have in these events.

The astronomers, to whom even the smallest celestial event was significant, must have been quaking in their sandals at what had happened. Three eclipses within a week's time. How often would that happen in history? Once in a million years? What is extraordinary is that a total solar eclipse, the most spectacular astronomical event witnessed by Earth inhabitants, happened at dawn.

The following illustration shows the positions of the Sun, Moon and Earth during a solar eclipse. Notice the small size of the Moon's shadow touching Earth.

4:1 SOLAR ECLIPSE

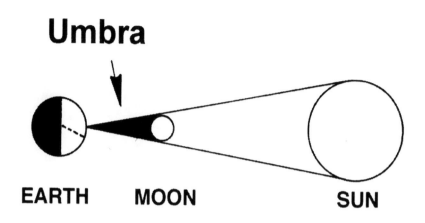

Umbra

EARTH   MOON   SUN

For the Sun to be seen as totally eclipsed by viewers on Earth, the darkest portion of the Moon's shadow (the umbra) must reach the surface of the Earth. The circular umbra touching Earth may reach up to 250-miles in diameter. The size of the umbra touching Earth depends upon the distance between the Moon and Earth. The closer the Moon is to Earth, the larger the umbra. Only those persons within the umbra will be able to see the total solar eclipse. Persons outside the umbra may see a partial solar eclipse.

EVENT # 6: SEPTEMBER 2, 0004 A.D.

FACT: The sixth significant event of Jesus' birth announcement began the next day, September 2, 0004, at sunrise when the Moon continued on its monthly journey. While moving westward, Saturn continued to separate from the Sun that had been eclipsing it. Mars and Venus were still in visible and brilliant opposition. For the next two weeks, brilliant Saturn,

Venus, and Mars continued to rise right before the Sun in the morning sky. Venus, in its smaller elliptical path, moved closer and closer to Saturn.

ANCIENT SYMBOLIC INTERPRETATION: As the Saturn god continued to rise in the sky, the ancient astronomers would make the interpretation that even though Saturn was subordinate to the new God, it would become as powerful as it was before the eclipsing event. Thus the new God would be mightier than Saturn ever was, or would be, and yet mightier than any of the other gods in the sky.

EVENT # 7: SEPTEMBER 15, 0004 A.D.

FACT: Right before sunrise, Venus was the brightest object in the sky. The seventh significant event of Jesus' birth announcement began at sunrise when Venus moved in front of Saturn and eclipsed that planet. At first it appeared to be a spectacular conjunction of the two planets as they appeared to fuse into one object in the morning sky. The spectacle of the Venus god blocking out the Saturn god created the fourth eclipse in this set of celestial events. This eclipse event took several days for Venus had to approach Saturn, move in front of the further planet to eclipse it, and continue on its way. Much of this time the two planets appeared to be a conjunction of two brilliant stars.

ANCIENT SYMBOLIC INTERPRETATION: The ancient astronomers would have interpreted this event to mean that the Saturn and Venus gods met in the sky to join in agreement to spectacularly announce the coming of the new God. Venus was brighter in the sky than it would be for many years to come. Saturn would not be that bright again until it orbited the Sun it its long path taking over twenty-nine years, more than the time of a human generation. The ancient astronomers believed their sky gods joined in commitment to the new God.

Saturn, ruler of the universe, was associated with fertility of the coming of spring and harvest. Venus was also a god of fertility. The five day joining of the two major gods of fertility affirmed the birth of the new God of creation. They had previously shown their subordinate positions to the new God. Creating a brilliant light, they helped celebrate and welcome the new, all powerful God. Saturn was once again illustrating he was the father of kings.

EVENT # 8: SEPTEMBER 20, 0004 A.D.

FACT: Venus and Saturn began to separate in the dawn sky. Within nine days, the Moon once more joined the group of planets and moved among them. The days of September 29th and 30th found brilliant Mars rising in the dark morning sky followed by Saturn, the Moon, Venus, and the Sun.

ANCIENT SYMBOLIC INTERPRETATIONS: Ancient astronomers believed the Moon god of knowledge joined the Venus and Saturn gods to show agreement and to celebrate the new King of the universe.

EVENT #9: OCTOBER 1, 0004 A.D.

FACT: The ninth significant event of Jesus' birth announcement took place at dawn on the first day of October, 0004 when the Moon eclipsed the Sun for the second time within thirty-days. Thus far in these events, a solar eclipse occurred on September 1st and then again one month later on October 1. The second eclipse was only a partial solar eclipse for the Moon did not totally cover the Sun. Therefore, to observers on Earth, part of the Sun remained visible. It was not only extremely unusual to have a partial and total solar eclipse of the Sun within two orbits of the Moon, but such an occurrence has not been witnessed since.

Making more of an impact during the solar eclipse, three bright objects were lined up in the sky at the same time, Venus, Saturn, and Mars. Both eclipses happened at dawn when the ancient astronomers took their celestial observations.

ANCIENT SYMBOLIC INTERPRETATION: To the astronomers in the year of Christ's birth, the Moon god of all knowledge again eclipsed the Sun. That this eclipse was a partial solar eclipse and a partial repeat of the eclipse of 30-days previously symbolically reaffirmed the subordinate nature of the Sun god to the new God. The Sun god was eclipsed twice in this set of birth announcements to shout out the might of the new God.

EVENT #10: NOVEMBER 20, 0004 A.D.

FACT: The tenth and last significant event of Jesus' celestial birth announcement took place beginning November 1, 0004 when Mars was no longer visible in the morning sky. Saturn rose higher at dawn while Venus dropped towards the horizon. By November 20th, Venus had disappeared during dawn while Saturn continued to climb within the ecliptic path, the path followed by what they called wandering stars.

ANCIENT SYMBOLIC INTERPRETATION: Saturn, the ruler of the universe, continued to rise in the sky to make the announcement concerning the location of the birth place of the

IRENE BARON

new God. As the astronomers watched Saturn, the father of the kings moved toward the west as they would have earlier predicted. In early December Saturn would have appeared to be almost over Bethlehem at daybreak. The astronomers, with their mathematics and planning, knew all these celestial events would happen and knew when and where they would all end. By going to the location below the Saturn god, they would find the birth place of the new Earth born God, just outside of Bethlehem.

Jesus Christ must have therefore been born in early December.

Any astronomer following the stars would naturally be expected to make a beeline for Bethlehem as they neared that location. For Mary to have given birth to Jesus east of Bethlehem would have made it easier for them to find the child as they would pass that location when arriving from the east. They would find the child in a lowly stable/cave and bring their treasures in homage. Men honored the God who was honoring them by being born on Earth.

Thus, the planet Saturn would have risen in the east at sunrise in September and over time moved westward by early December. At daybreak, when astronomers made their daily observations, Saturn would appear to be above or near Bethlehem. The astronomers would have followed the bright objects west to Bethlehem. With the rising Sun, the Moon caused solar eclipses, the antics of planets Jupiter, Mars, Saturn and Venus, the astrological signs were worthy for the birth of a new king and leader for mankind.

When the emissaries witnessed the might of Jesus Christ in His infant state in Bethlehem, they were the first Gentiles to worship Him. These influential leaders and their fellow travelers would take the awe of the new God back to their lands. Jesus Christ, perhaps, began to change the world with the opinions of those learned men.

69

To most people who lived at that time in history, all the objects in the sky, except for the Moon and Sun, were considered to be stars. The word "star" has always been in the descriptions of the Christmas star. In reality, the final beaconing "star," the tenth and last event in the heavenly birth announcement, was actually the planet Saturn.

The men who were the astronomers were perhaps also called the wisemen, wizards, magi, magicians, alchemists, emperors, and kings. They interpreted celestial events in ways we can observe from drawings and documents they left behind. From ancient temples and rock carved script, the civilizations from Egypt to China have given us clues as to how they would have interpreted celestial events.

These events are listed for Bethlehem in Judea, approximately 31-degrees 40-minutes North of the Equator and 35-degrees, 20-minutes east of the prime meridian. The events were found and verified using computer programs for six o'clock in the mornings for the year 4, A.D.

After surveying and studying astronomical events covering fifteen years of data, the year 4 was the only year the author found having significant celestial events occurring that were remarkable enough to proclaim witness to the coming God.

It is important to remember the ancient astronomers of the Babylonian, Assyrian, Egyptian, Indian, Persian, and Chinese civilizations used the predawn of the rising Sun for their astronomical observations. Readers attempting to verify this information on their home computers must use dawn as their start time.

Holy Bible. The King James Version. Galatians 4:4:

"But when the fullness of the time was come, God sent forth His Son.

Prophets hundreds of years before the birth of Jesus Christ wrote, as documented in the Old Testament of the *Holy Bible*, that God would send One in the "fullness" of time. That time came to Earth during the peaceful reign of Augustus Caesar from 31 B.C. to 14 A.D. Virgil called that age the "Messianic" as it was so predicted in early literature. People could travel about the Roman world with a high degree of safety and did so, for the Roman militia were based in all the provinces and quickly stopped any local conflicts. Those who broke the laws were punished. Jesus grew to age ten during the reign of Augustus Caesar. During the reign of Tiberius, 14 A.D. to 37 A.D., Jesus spent his youth, ministry, and was crucified.

This time in history is considered the perfect time for Jesus to have been born since persons could safely travel and move about. Christian missionaries could easily travel throughout the known world to spread the word of this rapidly growing religion of Christianity.

As mentioned, December 25th was set for the birthday of Jesus in the year 354 A.D. It was changed by agreement with converted Romans who realized, for the populous to change their religion, the seven day pagan celebrations held during the solstice had to be saved. The citizens looked forward to the pagan holidays. No new religion could remove their freedom of riotous celebrating. Their "Saturnalia" and "Sol Invictus" holidays took place when people celebrated the harvest. The Roman ruler, newly converted to Christianity, knew he had to have a substitute celebration for Saturnalia to get people to change, by his command, to Christianity.

Once the agreement was made, the date to celebrate the birth of Jesus Christ was changed within the month of December to coincide with the harvest and solstice celebrations. The citizens of Rome continued to keep the Sun worship along with their early Christianity. Many of the churches they built faced the sun.

The following illustrated celestial events in the birth announcements of Jesus Christ have been drawn from the original computer graphics. The mathematically precise astronomy computer programs were originally set to produce graphics for the celestial events above Bethlehem at six o'clock in the morning on the dates listed. The figures to the right hand side of each illustration represent the observers altitude beginning with the horizon at 0° altitude to Zenith at 90° altitude.

4:2 LEGEND COMPUTER GRAPHICS

OBJECT	LETTER SYMBOL	GRAPHIC SYMBOL
Moon	M	●
Sun	S	○
Mars	M	•
Venus	V	•
Saturn	S	◐

To use and understand the following computer illustrations, follow the directions listed below.

1. Place the illustration in front of you.

2. Place your hand or a blank paper over the illustration. The top of your palm/paper will represent the horizon

of the rotating Earth. Just as it happens every day, the Earth rotates toward the east.

3. Slowly move the top of your palm/paper down over the illustration. Imagine yourself observing the sky before dawn. As the palm/paper moves down, the first object you see drawn in the illustration is the first major object the ancient astronomers saw rise above the horizon in the East on that date. Continuing the downward motion, other objects appear in the same order as they were witnessed. They are separated as the ancient astronomers would have seen them distanced from one another in the sky.

4. When you reach the 0° altitude line, the bottom line, you will see the sky as it was at six o'clock in the morning for the listed date. The objects above it rose earlier in the day.

5. The Moon moves quickly in the sky compared to the other objects. Therefore its' exact position over minutes of time varies. For example, during a solar eclipse, the Moon would appear to cross the surface of the Sun in less than five minutes. When an eclipse is illustrated, try to imagine the movement of the Moon in front of the Sun. The other objects would have remained fairly stationary in comparison.

4:3 EVENT # 1

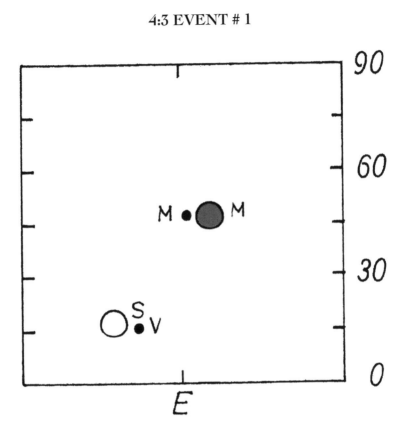

When the Sun rose for an hour to an altitude position of fifteen-degrees above the horizon, it was within a few degrees of Venus. Mars and the Moon were about one degree apart and about ten degrees east of the Sun. In elevation, they were halfway between the horizon and zenith.

4:4 EVENT #2

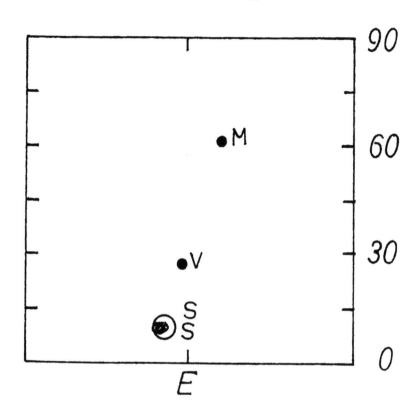

All three planets are at opposition and very brilliant. Mars rose three hours before the sun. Venus rose an hour before the Sun. Saturn rose in the sky after Venus. The moon was entering crescent phase. Shown in this illustration is the Sun with three brilliant shining planets above it in the dawning sky. It had caught up with Saturn and moved in front of it, eclipsing the planet. Saturn was to remain eclipsed by the Sun for four days.

4:5 EVENT #3

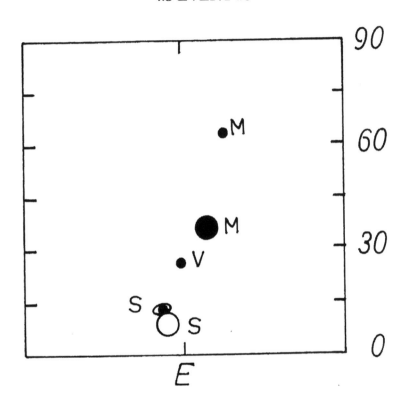

Before the Sun Mars rose in the sky followed by the Moon and Venus. When the Sun rose in the morning sky, the extremely bright Saturn became visible. The eclipse of Saturn was ending. There were five brilliant objects lined up in the sky They were in descending order: Mars, the Moon, Venus, Saturn and the Sun. Saturn moved westward toward the position where it would eventually pinpoint Bethlehem. Mars and Venus rose higher in altitude as the morning progressed.

4:6 EVENT #4

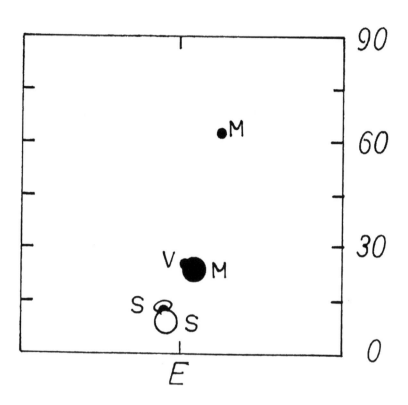

The upper sky containing Mars was still dark before the Sun's light reached it. As Venus rose above the horizon, the Moon moved in front of Venus and partially eclipsed it. Saturn was still emerging from being eclipsed by the Sun. Therefore, there were two partial eclipses visible at the same time.

4:7 EVENT #5

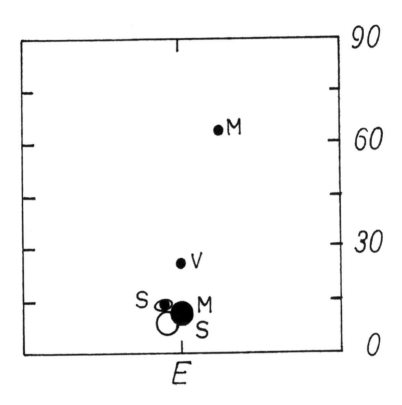

Mars rose into the dark sky before sunrise. Venus followed later. Shortly after sunrise the Moon totally eclipsed the Sun while the Sun was partially eclipsing the slow moving Saturn.

4:8 EVENT # 6

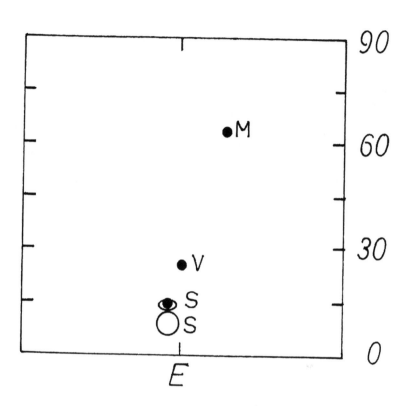

Mars rose first in the dark dawning sky. Venus rose second. While moving westward, Saturn continued to separate from the Sun that had been eclipsing it. For the next two weeks, brilliant Mars, Venus and Saturn continued to rise right before the Sun in the morning sky. Venus, in its smaller elliptical path, moved closer to Saturn.

4:9 EVENT # 7

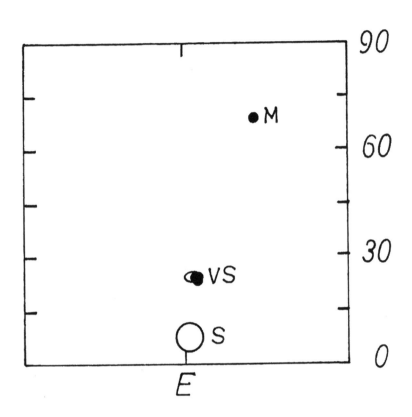

Mars rose first in the dark dawning sky. Venus rose second and was the brightest object in the sky. At sunrise Venus moved in front of Saturn and eclipsed that planet. At first it appeared to be a spectacular conjunction of the two planets as they appeared to fuse into one object in the morning sky. This eclipse event took several days for Venus had to approach Saturn, move in front of the further planet to eclipse it, and continue on its way. Much of this time they appeared to be a conjunction of two brilliant stars.

4:10 EVENT # 8

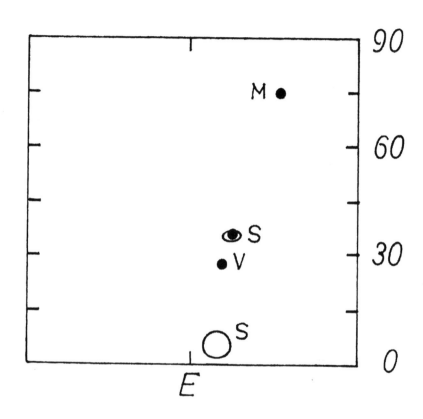

Venus and Saturn began to separate in the dawn sky. Within nine days, the Moon once more joined the group of planets and moved among them. The days of September 29th and 30th found brilliant Mars rising in the dark morning sky followed by (listed in order of their appearance) Saturn, the Moon, Venus, and the Sun.

4:11 EVENT #9

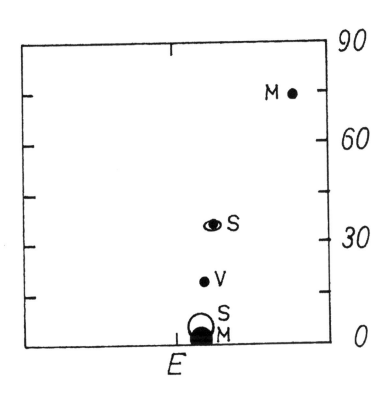

Mars rose into the dark sky before Saturn. Next came Venus. At sunrise, the Moon eclipsed the Sun for the second time within thirty-days. Since it was a partial eclipse, part of the Sun remained visible to Earth observers. Making more of an impact during the solar eclipse, three bright objects were lined up in the sky at the same time, Mars, Saturn and Venus.

4:12 EVENT #10

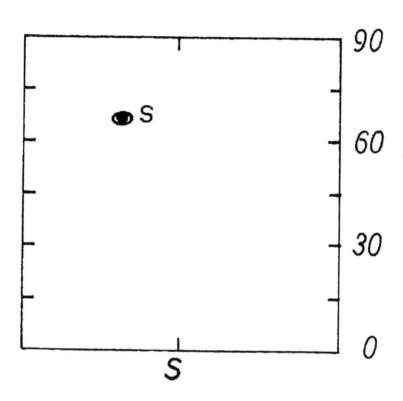

The tenth and last significant event of Jesus' birth announcement took place beginning November 1, 0004 when Mars was no longer visible in the morning sky. Saturn rose higher at dawn while Venus dropped towards the horizon. By November 20th, Venus had disappeared during dawn while Saturn continued to climb within the ecliptic path, the path followed by what they called wandering stars. It became the position marker showing the wisemen the geographical location of the Christ Child.

CHAPTER 5
The Wisemen

The Gospel of Matthew does not tell how many wisemen honored Jesus Christ at his birth place, but tradition has held the minimum number to three. At that time in history, once they arrived on that continental area, they had to travel by local animals such as horses or camels. By the Sixth Century names and origins had been hypothetically assigned to each wiseman. Who were the true wisemen with their supporting entourages? Matthew mentioned they were from the east. Exactly where in the east is not clear.

> *Holy Bible.* King James Version. Isaiah 60:1-9:
>
> 1 Arise, shine; for thy light is come, and the glory of the Lord is risen upon thee. 2 For behold, the darkness shall cover the earth, and gross darkness the people: but the Lord shall arise upon thee, and his glory shall be seen upon thee. 3 And the Gentiles shall come to thy light, and kings to the brightness of thy rising. 4 Lift up thine eyes round about, and see: all they gather themselves together, they come to thee: thy sons shall come from

far, and thy daughters shall be nursed at thy side. 5 Then thou shall see, and flow together, and thine heart shall fear, and be enlarged: because the abundance of the sea shall be converted unto thee, the forces of the Gentiles shall come unto thee. 6 The multitude of camels shall cover thee, the dromedaries of Midian and Ephah; all they from Sheba shall come: they shall bring gold and incense; and they shall shew forth the praises of the Lord. 7 All the flocks of Kedar shall be gathered together unto thee, the rams of Nebajoth shall minister unto thee: they shall come up with acceptance on mine altar, and I will glorify the house of my glory. 8 Who are these that fly as a cloud, and as the doves to their windows? 9 Surely the isles shall wait for me, and the ships of Tarshish first, to bring thy sons from far, their silver and their gold with them, unto the name of the Lord thy God, and to the Holy One of Israel, because He hath glorified thee.

The locations of these ancient places can be better understood by using modern maps in an atlas of the world. Kedar is now the area of northern or northwestern Saudi Arabia. Sheba is an ancient country in southern Arabia, just north of Southern Yemen, known for its spices and gems. The Midians are members of a desert tribe of northwest Arabia, near the **Gulf of Aqaba**, and descended from the fourth son of Abraham, the original Midian. Hphah is the mountainous Al Hi Jaz region of northwestern Saudi Arabia in which Al-Madinah (Medina) is located.

There are many lands to use in our speculation as to the origins of the wisemen. Could it be that one of the wisemen was of a race descended from an Egyptian court, perhaps living in Persia? The Egyptians, remember, knew the celestial sphere and believed the dawn risings of the Sun, Moon and stars told of their gods and goddesses being born, rejuvenated, or reincarnated. Many of the objects they used everyday had numerous meanings, but those of the Sun were most often worshipped and used, such as the circle and the ankh-shaped cross with the often imbedded circle.

Prior to Christ's birth, when so many significant celestial events appeared at once, the religious priests and royalty knew from their symbolism that a God was being born. The gods of their heaven were announcing the birth of the greatest God to exist since the Earth was created. Never in history had so many celestial objects appeared and performed at sunrise, the time of day most important for the astronomers.

Through their knowledge of heavenly movements, astronomers would have calculated such events were going to occur. Not only that they would occur, but how long it would take for each of the star gods to deliver their message using the heavens as their stage. As the objects moved across the sky, the astronomers could track and map motions. They must have felt impelled to seek the God whom these celestial events foretold.

The size of the events in the heavens was important. To have so many objects performing, converging, and eclipsing created brilliance in the morning sky which had not been seen in written history. The brilliance would have impacted the known world and been interpreted to be symbolic of power, importance, strength, glory, and divine intervention for the newborn God.

A member of the Egyptian royal family, living either in the Greek ruled Egypt or their adopted Persian land, most likely was one of the wisemen to have brought the gold presented to Mary and Joseph in Bethlehem. Gold was very important to that culture not only economically, but it represented their everlasting Sun god.

If the birth being foretold had been that of an ordinary prince or princess, a lone representative may have accomplished the honors for the country. For the birth child to be the greatest God in the whole universe, the ruler would not only be expected to visit in person, they wouldn't want to miss the opportunity to see this God for themselves. Who wouldn't want to be in the new God's presence for one moment in their life? Their curiosity would make this one of the most magnificent events in their life, for other than the Pharaohs of Egypt and the emperors of China, this great God was the only one to exist on Earth. All other gods resided in the sky.

By honoring the new God, the emissaries would bring respect to their kingdoms and perhaps prosperity for the future. A close alliance with the God would have been considered diplomatic, especially in the case of a future war. The different nations needed to "cover their bases."

To have the all important and forceful Sun god foretell the birth of the greatest God being born on Earth, only gold would be a gift worthy enough to present when the visiting emissary or king humbled himself. To honor another king, the greatest gift of pure gold, would have been presented. Therefore, why not give it also to the new God? Gold was believed to offer protection, even after death. Pharaohs, for example, had gold masks placed over their heads when buried in their chambers in order to represent their kinship with the gods of their beliefs. Tutankhamen even had a gold lined inner coffin. Gold leaf and inlay were added to objects of religious importance.

IRENE BARON

Gold is still considered a favorite of the gods. If you were to visit a current Buddhist temple in Asia, you would see Buddhist worshipers purchasing a small one-inch square of gold leaf to heat gently with the flame of a small candle. When hot enough, the gold leaf would be pressed against a statue of Buddha. The favorite statues glisten with the non-tarnishing metal while the givers of the gold receive honor in their march toward Nirvana, the Buddhist form of heaven.

What would an emissary visiting the birth of a new god have worn? He would have wanted to represent his country with all the pomp and formal circumstance possible. Even as he traveled, he would have worn luxurious robes as he did in his palace. He would have been carried by slaves, horses, or camels and had an entourage of astronomer guides, wise-men, priests, slaves, wives, concubines, cooks, and support personnel.

The blue color of the lapis lazuli mineral is between royal and navy blue. It is made more beautiful by the gold commonly laced within the gem. Because the blue represented the celes-tial sky and the gold represented the gods, the gem held much symbolism. Not common in Egypt, lapis had to be imported to that region.

An emissary visiting the greatest God of all gods would have dressed in a manner representative for meeting a celestial being. Lapis lazuli may have been the gem of preference as it was the dark blue of the early dawn. It is suggested a Egyptian or Persian emissary visiting Jesus' birthplace would have logi-cally worn lapis lazuli, often used in scarabs relating to the Sun and celestial objects. Some archaeologists believe that lapis was thought to be the substance of the hair and beards of the gods, another reason it was used when images of the gods were created of the gem. The tomb of Tutankhamen in Thebes in the Valley of the Kings had a lapis lazuli scarab pendant.

One Egyptian god, Amun, was called Lord of the Lapis Lazuli and painted in scenes with blue skin. Egyptian kings of the Eighteenth Dynasty were painted with blue faces to show their relationship to their celestial gods. One can only speculate whether a Persian wiseman, descended from Egyptians, painted his face yellow to represent the gold, or blue to represent the heavens, or not at all when presented to the new God. From the commonness of the painting of the skin by priests who colored their bodies, as witnessed by the Egyptian painted kings on the walls of the temples and burial sites, skin painting would not have been rare.

It is known that some priests wore white sandals while performing sacred temple work, so the emissary during the presentation of his gift to the new God may have worn the same. White symbolized white gold and depicted the Sun and Moon. Common to that time in history, sandals were adorned with carvings of white alabaster.

Alabaster, not common to much of north Africa, had to be imported. Created by grinding pure white marble into very fine microscopic, powdery fragments and cementing them together into any shape desired, it was often used for ceremonial bowls, goblets, and even tables upon which kings were laid for burial preparation after their deaths.

A helmet or headdress of gold, signifying the wearer was considered to be a holy ruler, was most likely worn at the presentation. White crowns were originally an emblem of kings of southern Egypt. Lower priests following in the old religious traditions in the presentation would have worn sashes of gold and lapis, gold aprons, and wide gold bracelets from which dangled more offerings. Gold bracelets, covering the forearm area and depicted in ancient artwork, numbered at least three from elbow to wrist, with one over the hand.

How would the gift of gold have been presented to the family of Jesus Christ? Most likely on trays of white alabaster for white was symbolic of cleanliness and all things sacred and pure.

If traditions portrayed on ancient paintings were followed, the gold bearer would have his arms parallel and extended in front of him. Upon his arms would lay the alabaster or lapis tray upon which the true gifts rested. At the corners and along the edges, the tray would have gold trim. The gifts, as shown in temple paintings, were contained in woven gold baskets of different ornate forms. The Egyptian term meaning "generosity" was traditionally represented by an extension of the hand, perhaps cupped upwards.

In one representative painting, a temple relief from the Eighteenth Dynasty presently located in the Cleveland Museum of Art in northern Ohio, one gold basket was drawn and painted showing eight construction splints. As common Egyptian art showed one-half of any object drawn, it can be easily assumed the whole basket had sixteen splints around it with eleven weaves of gold and one gold band around the top circumference covering the edges of the splint weave.

There is evidence of a gold band of trim around the bottom of the basket. The height of the baskets was approximately one-half the distance from the elbow to the shoulder of the person presenting the offering, making it about six to seven-inches tall. The top diameter of the basket was proportionally identical to the height. The basket base was one-half the height, or three and one half inches. The first basket in the painting was overflowing with gold objects arranged in a domed shape. Each object, perhaps of pure gold, had a rounded top much like an egg, but with a cylindrical base.

A second gold basket, relatively the same size and proportion of the first, had a diagonal weave of alternating gold and lapis colors. The lapis gem may have been imbedded into the gold. An example for such an inlaid design is on display at the

Zanesville Art Center in central Ohio. It resembles the technique currently used in India where ivory and mother-of-pearl are inlaid into rosewood. Each diagonal lapis splint of the basket was separated by one gold splint.

This second basket had a gold handle which was centered and vertical, higher than the base of the basket was wide. The wide trays bearing the gold baskets covered the presenters arms from the elbows to beyond the hands which were cupped under the tray, palms upward. The gifts offered to the child God were probably offered in gold baskets resting on white alabaster trays and carried by priests following the emissary.

An important question must have been whether the emissary would offer the gift of gold himself or have his priests make the presentations. Which situation would most honor the Christ Child and the emissary's home country?

While the gift of gold was being presented to the Christ child, incense was probably being burned by priests in the belief that gods revealed themselves not only by sight, but by smell. In their homelands, the most beautiful smells were interpreted as a manifestation of the god for whom the incense had been burned. It had also been representative of something both the mortal and immortal gods would experience, a commonality.

In their homelands, incense was offered in front of statues of gods in ancient religious proceedings, just as it is in present day temples and churches around the world. In addition to incense, the gifts of gold may have been sufficient to have seen Mary and Joseph out of the country during their trials with Herod and would have helped maintain their family during the years of exile.

The emissaries to Christ had time to discuss, debate, and plan their presentation for several years in advance of the event. They had to make sure they allowed a year or more for travel time, depending upon the distance they had to cover between their homeland and the birthplace of the God located under the position star.

Imagine the preparations which took place the actual day of their visit to the greatest God to ever exist in the universe. They would have prepared their bodies, being cleansed and rubbed with the finest oils and perfumes, dressed with the finest robes, jewels, and headdresses. Their entire entourage would have been bedecked with refinements of which we can only dream. The camels, horses, and beasts of burden would have been draped with the colors and gems of celestial gods to show respect for the newly born God.

The emissaries would have wanted to ensure that how they looked, what they wore, what gifts they offered, and how they presented the gifts were perfect. In anticipation, they must have consulted every priest and knowledgeable person of their kingdom for advice before leaving on their journey to follow the position marking star. Ruling emissaries would have known that their own birth was nothing in comparison to that of the new God, before which they were humbled.

Following the protocol of their countries, the emissaries would bow, kneel, or lie down on the ground in adoration or submission before the newborn God. Ancient paintings show priests touching the knees or grasping their shoulders to create a cross of the arms.

Other paintings show priests holding their arms in front of them shoulder height, palms toward the person/king/god they are honoring with the thumbs pointing down. Kneeling with this same arm and hand position supposedly intensified the supplication. In complete prostration, lying flat on the ground, is probably how the emissaries most likely approached the child, trembling as they did so, knowing the power and import of the God so born. They expected this child would rule the whole universe as no one before Him.

Through their writings, Luke and Matthew created a celebrity site in Bethlehem which lies on an important traffic artery leading south to Hebron. At that time in history it would have been crowded with or without the concentration of returning citizens to their homeland as required by the census.

There are many arguments as to where Jesus was born, in a cave or stable. The present Church of the Nativity at Bethlehem may have been rebuilt numerous times and is one of the most ancient churches of Christendom. Stairways leading down to a cave grotto are thirty-three feet long by thirteen feet wide. Perhaps it had been a stable in a cave.

Holy Bible. King James Version. Micah 4:8:

And thou, O tower of the flock, the strong hold of the daughter of Zion, unto thee shall it come, even the first dominion; the kingdom shall come to the daughter of Jerusalem.

East of Bethlehem is a "tower of Eder," or Migdal-eder, which means "tower of the flock." The prediction that the kingdom of the daughter of Jerusalem was to come to that tower may be a reference to the angel of God announcing to the shepherds of the nearby village of Midgal-eder the birth of Jesus, or to Mary, the daughter of Jerusalem.

Five hundred years before the birth of Jesus, the word 'Bethlehem" meant "House of the god Lehem." Lehem, a deity also named "Lahmu," was responsible for giving the rains necessary for life, especially in the desert.

Holy Bible. King James Version. Micah 5:2:

But thou, Bethl-ehem Ephratah, though thou be little among the thousands of Judah, yet

out of thee shall He come forth unto me that is to be ruler in Israel; whose goings forth have been from of old, from everlasting.

Is interesting to note that Bethlehem Ephratah is the area where Rachel was buried by the roadside with a pillar erected on her grave. The pillar had been given the name, "the pillar of the tomb of Rachel." As shepherds took their sheep to that area, it was also called the "tower of the flock."

In the old world of Bethlehem, there may have been an Ephratah or other outlying settlement of somewhat similar name in the immediate vicinity. Over the years the names may have changed as towns crumbled to dust. It is fairly certain to scholars that the Christmas shepherds were located in the region of Rachel's tomb.

The emissaries must have wondered about the origin of a God born in a lowly cave-like stable outside the centuries old town of Bethlehem. They had to question the symbolism of such a humble beginning. They most likely expected Him to have been born in a magnificent palace or temple.

To witness the conditions of Christs' birth place would have caused them to question their own extravagant life styles in comparison. They would have critically evaluated the splendor and necessity of their own palaces and temples.

If the greatest event on Earth began with the greatest God being born in such dire circumstances, what must this have meant to nations that thrived on symbolism? To nations where shapes, sounds, smells, Suns, and stars all symbolized something which altered life on Earth and Earth itself, what must one God of all existence being born in a lowly stable have symbolized? What meanings must this have imparted to the kings, designated emissaries, priests or entourages? All of the arguments, discussions, and interpretations of the new God upon return to their homelands can only be imagined. They saw the new God of the universe needed none of the pomp and circumstance previously considered necessary and commonplace.

The God of the universe required only His existence.

What an impact this must have made on the priests who formerly believed their earthly ruler-gods the most important beings on the planet. The eminence of Jesus Christ began to impact His universe.

Those traveling to honor the new God must have wondered what the offspring of such a true God would be like and what preparations should be made for the descendents. They probably assumed that the descendants of this God would eventually number into the tens of thousands, for He would most likely produce offspring to populate the Earth. They could not have known the God they were to honor during their visit was to be sacrificed before He had any direct descendents.

CHAPTER 6
Computer Evidence

The June 16, 1962 issue of *Science News* reported that Dr. O. Neugebauer of Brown University, Providence, R.I used computer calculations for positions of the planets, the moon and the sun. He took the mathematical computer calculations as far back as 601 B.C. Dr. Neugebauer was the first person reported to have used the computer analysis programs for ancient astronomical records. Since that time, other amateur and professionals have used computers to study the heavens.

Most present day astronomers using computers to calculate astronomical phenomena associated with the birth of Jesus Christ have done so using the time frame between sunset and midnight. They did not take into account the fact that ancient astronomers used pre-dawn and dawn observations. Much that has been published prior to this book had little bearing on the true Christmas star event.

Computers can be used to reliably calculate the positions of celestial objects for thousands of years when the programs are written correctly. This is due to the fact that the movements of the Moon, Earth, planets, Sun, and stars are mathematically precise.

Previous astronomers were looking for one fantastic Christmas event, not realizing that a multitude of events brought the wisemen following the progression of dawn events moving east to west. What is critical to this study is proof of the culminating event occurring right over the position of Bethlehem.

When I used sunrise as the time frame, no matter how far backward or forward the programs were run, the several months of events that document Jesus' birth according to ancient interpretations of the events cannot be overlooked. That they culminated right over Bethlehem was the final clue that this time frame was correct. What other celestial events occurred at the correct right ascension and declination over Bethlehem? None that I could find. I surveyed approximately 15-years of events during more than two years of sitting in front of computers.

The brilliant heavenly events moving in the sky toward Bethlehem were interpreted by the ancient astronomers, astrologers, priests, magi, and wisemen as the birth announcement of the greatest God of their universe. The Hebrew name of the new God was "Yeshua", which meant "Yahweh (God) is savior (helper)". In other languages, it became "Iesous" and finally the English "Jesus".[1] The word "Christ" was added after he was anointed.

Computers cannot calculate open spaces. They must have designated beginning and ending points or lines to compute data. Earth's surface has been divided into latitude and longitude lines for purposes of measurement. These imaginary lines can be used by computers. Latitude lines are the imaginary lines that are drawn around the globe in an east-west direction. The largest latitude line is the equator.

The latitude of the equator, a great circle that cuts the Earth into two fairly equal portions halfway between the northern and southern poles, rests at 0-degrees latitude. Moving north of the equator, the latitude increases in degrees until reaching the geographic north pole at 90-degrees north. The extension of latitude lines into space enables one to mark off the celestial sphere by degrees of "declination." The line in space extending from the equator is 0° declination. The declination of stars over Bethlehem is 31°43'0" north.

The next time you see a globe representing Earth, imagine the latitude and longitude lines extending out into space. These lines are what the computers use to determine positions in space above the surface of the Earth.

In Illustration 6:1, if you placed the center of a protractor on the point at the center of the Earth and placed the degree starting line at the equator, you would see how the latitude of Bethlehem was measured. The north pole makes a 90° angle (right angle) from the center of the earth towards the north while the south pole makes a 90° angle (right angle) toward the south.

The imaginary longitude lines around the surface of the Earth are drawn from the North Geographic Pole(GNP) to the South Geographic Pole (GSP). Measurements of longitude are made beginning with the first longitude line. That line is numbered 0°-longitude and is called the prime meridian. It cuts through the English village of Greenwich. The citizens of Greenwich have the prime meridian painted up the sides of houses, over the roofs and down onto the sidewalks and streets across the village. A tourist attraction, when viewed from the air it appears as a straight yellow line cutting across the town.

All longitude lines up to 180° –west of the prime meridian are designated as west longitude. Those up to 180° –east of the prime meridian are designated as east longitude. The longitude line where they meet half way around the Earth is called the International Date Line.

The north-south axis of the celestial sphere is mapped using an extension of the Earth's longitude lines. Each longitude line extends from Earth to the end of the universe. They are named "right ascension" (RA).

Astronomy computer programs using the correct right ascension and declination were used to obtain data and answers during this research study. The early programs from NASA were received on plain black, square, floppy disks with few or no markings on the outside of the disks except for the typed names of the programs each contained.

Some of the computer programs tried to limit the years in which I could research data. For example, some would only go back 1,500-years, and not the 2,000-years needed. When searching for data to verify what was found by comparing computer programs, I discovered some programs, upon reaching their limit, would request how many hours forward or backward I wished from that limited date.

Using a calculator, I determined the number of hours in one day rounded off to 24 (from the more exact 23-hours, 56-minutes, 4.6-seconds). By multiplying 24 by 365.25, the number of days in a year. I calculated there were 61,362 hours in a year.

6:1 LATITUDE

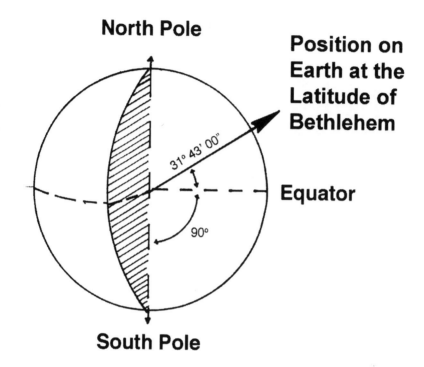

North Pole

Position on Earth at the Latitude of Bethlehem

31° 43' 00"

Equator

90°

South Pole

This shows a wedge of Earth removed to illustrate the position of the center of the earth. The dashed line around the Earth and through the center of the planet represents the position of the equator. The angle between the equator and the current Bethlehem latitude position is easily measured to be 31° 43' 00".

I then determined how many hours had lapsed since Jesus' birth using the date originally calculated for the year 0004. If I had reached the limit, the program requested how many hours forward or backward in time I wished to add or subtract from the assigned time. I multiplied 61,362 by however many more years I needed to back up the program and entered that data.

While working, I found the computer would behave as though frozen. I would wait three or four hours and nothing would happen. I formed the hypothesis that if I tried to calculate data beyond the program limits for a shorter period of time, I could tell if the program was actually working. If the program worked, it would take less time to perform the functions and show a screen of results.

Using this hypothesis, when applied and tested for a year or two back in time beyond a program limit, the computer began to show results in less than an hour. I knew the program was working. I just waited for the computations to be completed.

These programs took much time, but at least the screen would show the status such as "now doing calculations for Venus," to give me solace and patience. It was frustrating when I didn't know if a program was working and calculations were quietly taking place or if the computer was "frozen". I hesitated to reboot the computer by pressing control, alternate and delete buttons for I might have interrupted hours of data calculations that would have to be repeated.

The next problem encountered was that of being able to print the data. I finally installed a "Print-It" card with a command button. The Print-It button was used to print what appeared on the computer monitor as it came up during any program. When the red Print-It button was pushed, whatever was on the screen remained on the screen as the program was frozen at that point. By pressing return, the screen data was dumped to a printer which printed whatever was showed on the computer monitor as the program ran the data. The printer would print the requested data with over 50-sheets of figures for one set of calculations.

I would set the calculations in the program, press the Print-It button, and leave the machine alone. Twelve or more hours later, when the computer completed the calculations, it would begin to print the data.

When the printer paper would get stuck, some projects had to be repeated. Working with continuous paper and a some-times cantankerous printer, it sometimes took several tries and many hours of waiting to print the data from one request.

I also ran the NASA programs using the latitude and lon-gitude of Greenwich, England. The time zones and data would then be calculated east to Bethlehem.

One NASA disk offered the programs "Sunrise/Sunset/ Sun" locator, "Moonplotter" for phases and locations, planet **orbits**, planet coordinates, planet data, star and nebular loca-tors, rise/set/transit and star time and a planet orbit plotter for different solar masses. Other programs distributed by NASA gave the direction and time of Moon rise, the percent illumina-tion, the phase, position of Earth and the Moon and Sun.

Additional disks offered data programs on the solar system, astrophotography, and planetary features. Others found dates of Moon phases and eclipses, right ascension and declination for the Moon and planets, the rise and transit set of planets of the solar system, data about Mercury and Venus, the opposi-tions of Mars, and the time of twilight at any location. I used many programs in order to find additional coordinates for the Moon and planets. I compiled many sets of data of the same phenomena for comparison.

Coordinates were given for local, **civil, nautical** and **astronomical times**. When asked for planet data, the pro-grams gave the apparent size of the planet, the distance in Astronomical Units from the Sun (1 Astronomical Unit or 1 AU=93,000,000 miles), the angular distance from the Sun in degrees, and the angular diameter of the planet at conjunction with the Sun.

I had to compare what happened in the sky with the symbols, symbolism and ancient interpretations of the events. If the ancient interpretations had nothing to do with a birth, the information was ignored. After many searches and trials, the final dates I reinvestigated for clarification were July through December of the year 4.

There were some graphic programs that would not print. In those instances, I taped transparent, acetate sheets against the glass monitor and transferred the data to the acetate with markers. Some tables that wouldn't print were copied in longhand using pen or pencil. The right ascension and declination for each planet for the dates required were written from the "Planet Coordinates" program to confirm data.

A NASA program called the "Astro Almanac" was used to obtain the years, months, days, and **magnitude**s of lunar eclipses and phases for all the months of the years surrounding the birth of Jesus Christ.

Easy to read programs used graphics showing the positions of the planets at each occasion with a legend for each planet on the diagram. I ran programs several times to ensure that the data was printing correctly and that it came up the same each time.

I used "The Moon Finder" for GMT. It provided data about the Moon including right ascension, declination, azimuth, and elevation. The" Public Domain Astronomy #1" set of computer programs used from NASA was made up of many subsections including: "Astronomy Exposures, Conjunction, Equinoxes and Solstices, Lunar Eclipse Umbra, Moon Finder, Moon Phase Program, Moon Phases, Perpetual Calendar I, A Perpetual Calendar II, Planet Locator, Planet Views, Solar Eclipse I, Solar Eclipse 2, Solar system Orrery (mechanical model of the Solar system), Summing Stellar Magnitudes, Sun Azimuth, Sunrise Sunset, Sunrise/Set, Sunrise/Set Version 2, Time Dilation, Ursa Star Time and Year Sunrise/Set."

Another program used extensively was "Ephemeris Computer" to determine planet right ascensions and declinations in degrees, minutes and seconds for the months, days and years requested. The program listed the distances of the planets in Astronomical Units, AU.

To understand how the general population understood astronomy two-thousand years ago, think back to when you were a child. Did you ever sit outside with your family on a summer eve after dinner to watch the sunset and the arrival of the stars on the clear night? Do you remember the first star you saw at night as you watched the sunset? Often someone would recite the poem, "Star bright, star light, first star I've seen to night, wish I may, wish I might, have the wish I wish tonight." Then you or those around you would make a wish on the light of the first star. Did you ever wonder why your wishes never came true? What first appeared in the night sky was not a star, but in all probability, the planet Venus.

Advanced as we are scientifically, very few persons of today ever take astronomy classes and fewer yet venture outside with their astronomy teacher, as did my students during the 30-years I taught astronomy. Until taught to tell the difference, students couldn't tell planets from stars. To know where the ecliptic path of the planets lies through the star field would help persons distinguish stars from planets. A clue I gave my students was that planets don't twinkle. The twinkling of stars increases with the velocity of winds.

Is it any wonder that the people of the ancient world seeing a bright object in the sky assumed it to be a star? Like people of today, they couldn't tell a star from a planet.

Prior to and during Jesus' lifetime, astronomers were not taught in a school, but as apprentices in temples. The ruling officials did not have the astronomical knowledge necessary to tell one star from another or even learn the constellations. They left that up to the learned astronomers.

Since the ancients called every pinpoint of light a star, they called the planets stars. Thus the term was not "Christmas planet" but "Christmas star." They never knew the difference.

Who in your local, state, or national government offices knows much about astronomy? Those in the Senate or Congress? The President? The Vice President in the United States may reside in his official residence at the U.S. Naval Observatory. Due to that fact the Vice President may have more astronomy knowledge than other politicians. Most of your leaders, however, most likely do not know the difference between Venus and a star. So it was in Roman times. If a leader such as Herod had to know something about astronomy, they would call upon an expert.

My experts during research for this book were mathematical astronomy computer programs, science journals, research reports, and books by archaeologists, astronomers, and historians as noted in my reference section.

By having read through the material presented in this book you have hopefully learned what multiple computer programs have calculated concerning the heavenly birth announcement for Jesus Christ.

The actual position marker Christmas star was the last in a series of events announcing the birth of the greatest God in the Universe. The first nine events were the heavenly birth announcements. The last event showed the geographical location of the birth.

The ancient astronomers used the position of their Saturn god in that last event to determine the location of the birth. They probably didn't care if the birth took place in a town, city or open country. They were heading for the coordinates shown by their Saturn god. That the coordinates were near or in the town of Bethlehem was incidental to them.

Yes, there was a "Christmas star!"

CHAPTER 7
Computer Programs

The titles of the programs received for public domain use from the National Aeronautics and Space Administration (NASA) included:

Adjust Right Ascension & Declination for Precession
Altitude Azimuth
Altazimuth Calculator – Interpolator
Angular separation – Two Stars
Calendar
Calendrics
Close Encounters
Comet
Coordinates: Moon & Planets – Any Date
Conjunction
Dynamic Planet Orbit Plotter for different Solar Masses
Elongations & Transits of Polaris
Ephemerides
Ephemeris
Ephemeris computer
Equinoxes & Solstices
Galilean Satellite Positions
Great Circle Distance

Julian Day & Calendar Interchange
Lunar Eclipse/Umbra
Lunar & Solar Eclipse Calculations
Mars: Next Opposition & Data
Messier and NGC Catalogs
Moon: Eclipses for Any Year
Moon Finder
Moon: Phases for Any Date
Moon Phase Program
Moon Phases
Moon Plotter for Phases/Locations
North Sky: A Computerized Star Chart
Northern Star field
Observer
Planet Coordinates
Planet Data
Planet Finder
Planet Grand Tour
Planet Locator and Solar System Simulator
Planet Orbits
Planet views
Precession
RA & DEC ;Moon & Planets – Any Date
Retrograde Motion of Mars
Rise/Set/Transit & Star Time
Satellite Passage
Solar Eclipse #1
Solar Eclipse #2
Solar System Orrery
Solar system: Rise Transit Set
Spirografix – True Path Plotter
Star & Nebula Locator
Summing Stellar Magnitudes

Sun Azimuth & Maximum Altitude
Sunrise/Set
Sunrise/Set Version #2
Sunrise Sunset, Dawn & Dusk
Sunrise/Sunset/Sun locations
Text
Time Dilation
Time: Local Mean == Sidereal
Times of rising and Setting of Mercury and Venus
For Any Date
Twilight times: any Location
Ursa Star Time
Year Sunrise/Set & Twilight Calculator
Zodiac Sunsigns

Private program :

TellStar – Your Computer Graphics Window to the Universe. Spectrum
Holo Byte. 1982-1998. (Scharf Software Systems, Inc., Suite
1068. 2111-M 30th Street, Boulder, Colorado 80301.)

Endnotes

INTRODUCTION

1. Krupp, E. "Ancient Watchers of the Sky." *1980 Science Year.* World Book Science Annual. Chicago: World Book – Childcraft International. 9B-113. 1979.

2. Huber, R.V. *The Bible Through the Ages.* Readers Digest. New York. 1996.

3. Lyons, A. *Predicting The Future.* Harry N. Abrams, Inc. New York. 1990.

4. Drake, N. "In The News: Astronomers celebrate as star goes boom in neighborhood." *Science News.* September 24. 5-9. 2011.

5. Lyons, A. *Predicting The Future.* Harry N. Abrams, Inc. New York. 1990.

BIBLICAL RECORDS

1. Thompson, R.C. editor. Volume II. The Reports of The Magicians and Astrologers of Nineveh and Babylon. Luzac & Co. London. 1990.

2. Lyons, A. *Predicting The Future.* Harry N. Abrams, Inc. New York. 1990.

BASIC ASTRONOMY

1. Wilson, C. *Starseekers*. Doubleday & Company. New York. 1980.

2. Schaefer, B. "Heavenly Signs". *New Scientist*. December 21/28. 48-51. 1991

3. Huber, R.V. *The Bible Through the Ages*. Readers Digest. New York. 1996.

4. Krupp, E. *Archaeoastronomy and the Roots of Science*. AAAS Selected Symposium 71. Westview Press. Boulder, CO 1984.

5. Hamblin, D.J. *The First Cities*. Time Life Books. New York. 1973.

6. Mahdy, C. *Mummies, Myth and Magic in Ancient Egypt*. Thames & Hudson. Spain. 1989.

7. Lyons, A. *Predicting The Future*. Harry N. Abrams, Inc. New York. 1990.

8. Chaisson, ZE. McMillan, S. *Astronomy Today*. Prentice Hall, Englewood Cliffs, New Jersey. 1993.

9. Wilson, C. *Starseekers*. Doubleday & Company. New York. 1980.

10. North, J. *The Norton History of Astronomy & Cosmology*. W.W. Norton & Co., New York, N.Y. 1995.

11. Thuan Trinh Xuan. *The Secret Melody and Man Created the Universe*. Oxford University Press. New York. 1995.

12. Lyons, A. *PredictingThe Future*. Harry N. Abrams, Inc. New York. 1990.

13. Krupp, E.C. *Echos of the Ancient Skies: The Astronomy of Lost Civilizations*. Harper & Row Publishers, Inc. New York, New York. 1983.

14. Wilson, C. *Starseekers*. Doubleday & Company. New York. 1980.

15. Thompson, R.C. editor. Volume II. The Reports of The Magicians and Astrologers of Nineveh and Babylon. Luzac & Co. London. 1990.

16. Krupp, E.C. *Echos of the Ancient Skies: The Astronomy of Lost Civilizations.* Harper & Row Publishers, Inc. New York, New York. 1983.

17. Ibid.

18. Wilson, C. *Starseekers.* Doubleday & Company. New York. 1980.

19. Lyons, A. *Predicting The Future.* Harry N. Abrams, Inc. New York. 1990.

20. North, J. *The Norton History of Astronomy & Cosmology.* W.W. Norton & Co., New York, N.Y. 1995.

21. Wilson, C. *Starseekers.* Doubleday & Company. New York. 1980.

22. Ibid.

23. Lyons, A. *Predicting The Future.* Harry N. Abrams, Inc. New York. 1990.

ANCIENT SYMBOLISM

1. Mendelssohn, K. *The Riddle of the Pyramids.* Praeger Publishers. New York. 1974

2. Dixon, R. *Dynamic Astronomy.* Prentice Hall, Englewood Cliffs. 1989.

3. Mahdy, C. *Mummies, Myth and Magic in Ancient Egypt.* Thames & Hudson. Spain. 1989.

4. Kramer, S. & Editors of Time Life Books. *Great Ages of Man: Cradle of Civilization.* Time Inc. New York. 1967.

5, Krupp, E.C. *Echos of the Ancient Skies: The Astronomy of Lost Civilizations.* Harper & Row Publishers, Inc. New York, New York. 1983.

6. Schaefer, B. "Heavenly Signs." *New Scientist.* December 21/28. 48-51. 1991

7. Dixon, R. *Dynamic Astronomy.* Prentice Hall, Englewood Cliffs. 1989.

8. Dunn, R., Abrahamse, D., Davison, G., Farmer, E., Garvey, J., McNeill, W., Schillings, 3D.Victor, D. *A World History: Links Across Time & Place.* McDougal, Littell & Company. 1988.

THE CHRISTMAS STAR EVENTS

1. Evans, D. *The Wrong Way Comet and Other Mysteries of Our Solar System.* TAB Books. l Blue Ridge Summit. Pennsylvania. 1992.

Glossary

Abacus: Instrument used in mathematical calculations using sliding beads on wires to represent decimal places; believed to have originated in Babylonia.

Albedo: Refers to the percent of sunlight reflected from a planet or Moon.

Annular Eclipse: When at apogee and appearing smaller than the sun, a ring of the suns' photosphere surface appears around the Moon during a solar eclipse.

Asians: Inhabited lands extending from Poland to Siberia.

Assyrians: Originated from the Subartu district in northern Babylonia.

Astrologer: Believes positions of objects in the sky influence humankind,

Astronomer: In ancient times known as an alchemist, astrologer, astronomer, magi, magician, mathematician, priest, wiseman, or wizard, depending upon their repertoire of actions.

Navigational maps show evidence of astronomy observations by 13,000 B.C.

Astronomical Time: Refers to the time of day at the Royal Greenwich Observatory in Greenwich, England at the Prime Meridian. This is the clock time used for military and important international events. It is often called Greenwich Mean Time (GMT) and Universal Time (UT).

Babylonians: Believed the Sun, Moon and visible planets were homes of the gods. The planets were assumed to be strongest when rising or near zenith and weakest in retrograde motion.

Black Hole: Theoretically, a black hole may result from an exploding, super massive star. Through the mutual pull of gravity on all particles of matter, the material not escaping into space contracts into a single point at the gravitational center, a singularity. The gravitation field is so strong; there is no space left between subatomic particles.

Celestial: Pertaining to objects beyond the surface of the Earth, such as the Moon, Sun, stars and planets.

Chinese: By 700 B.C. the Chinese had accurate astronomy records from their dawn observations believing the knowledge of astronomy gave power over man and nature and should be kept from ordinary persons. The emperor was regarded as the base of the north celestial pole, holding all power on Earth to create stability and order.

Civil Time: Refers to time scales designated by governments for household, business, and other clock time.

Clock drive: The clock drive mechanism moves the telescope to keep the centered object in the correct alignment. Set for your latitude, the motion of the clock drive counteracts the Earth's rotation.

Conjunction: Objects appear to merge.

Cosmologist: Philosopher trying to explain how the universe originated and exists.

Cosmos: Refers to the universe.

Decan: Objects found within each 10-degree segment of a 360-degree circle.

Divination: To discover what is obscure or to foretell future events by supernatural means.

Eclipse: Occurs when a closer object blocks the view of a more distant object.

Ecliptic: Equator of the Sun extended outward to create a 360-degree plane in which the known planets of our Solar System travel.

Egypt: Second oldest civilization after Sumer dating to 3100 B.C. having over 800-gods and goddesses.

Equinox: Two times during the year direct rays of the Sun strike Earth's equator resulting in days with twelve hours of daylight and twelve hours of darkness. "Equi" means equal and "nox" means night.

Frankincense: An aromatic gum resin from trees which grew primarily in Somalia, the southern Arabian Peninsula region of Yemen, and Jordan. During the time of Christ frankincense was used for religious and medicinal purposes. Currently it is used for incense, fumigants and perfumes.

Gnomon: Section of the sundial that casts a shadow. Can be used to determine noon and the north direction.

Gulf of Aqaba: Eastern gulf of the red Sea.

Ishtar: Babylonian name for Venus.

Jesus: Son of Joseph. Known as Anointed of the Lord, Christ, Christ the Lord, Counselor, Lord, Saviour, Everlasting Father, Immanuel, Lamb of God, Lord, Lord God, Messiah, Prince of Peace, Son of David, Son of God, Son of the Highest, Wonderful, Mighty God, Jeshua (Dead Sea Scrolls), Jehoshua & Yeshua (Hebrew), Jahshua (India), Yuz Asaf (Northwest India), Iesous & Jesus (Greek), Iesus & Jesu (Latin), Yeshu (Issa (Sanskrit/Arabic), Yuza (Persian), and Jesus (English).

Jupiter: Largest planet yet found in our solar system. In ancient history, known as a god who created Earth, the natural laws within the universe, and holder of all astronomical knowledge.

Kedar: Refers to Arabia.

Illuminate: To shine by reflected sunlight.

Magi: The original name of a Magus is from Zoroastrianism priests of Persia. Considered wise in all things pertaining to gods, elements and astronomy, they were held in awe by the ignorant masses and given considerable political power. Other names attributed to them were alchemist, astrologer, astronomer, magician, mathematician, priest, wiseman, and wizard. In the days of the Chaldeans and Babylonians, they were healers, prophets, and keepers of knowledge. Later tradition called them kings. The Christian church honors the Bethlehem visitors as the first Gentiles to believe in Christ as God and celebrates their visit by the Feast of Epiphany. Marco Polo reported he visited the graves of three magi near Tehran. One hundred years earlier a Roman emperor stated he had moved their bodies to a German cathedral for protection.

Magnitude: In astronomy, a measure of brightness. The human eye can see stars no dimmer than 6th magnitude.

Marduk Temple: Raised as a link between heaven and earth; it was restored many times after the ravages of wars and was the largest of all the Babylonian temples covering over 60-acres. It is said to be the home of the tower of Babel.

Megalith: A prehistoric astronomical monument, some of which are great circles of stone like Stonehenge. Almost all have sighting lines to observable dawn astronomical events.

Melting Pot: Egypt may have been the original melting pot of races. Art work shows skins of many colors; art from the son of Cheops shows his blonde queen with blue eyes. The Rameses II mummy had yellow hair.

Mesopotamia: Ruled by Persian kings beginning 700 B.C. The period prior to Christ's birth, 323-141 B.C. is called the Seleucid period which used the cuneiform script to write. They took dawn astronomical observations from the top of ziggurats, the high pyramidal temples in the center of their cities.

Myrrh: A bitter tasting gum resin with much aroma obtained from the bark of the *Commiphora Myrrha* tree, a plant native to northeast Africa. Grown in Ethiopia and Yemen, myrrh was used in incense, perfume, cosmetics and medicine. The Egyptians used it to embalm dead bodies, filling them with the powdered resin. Currently it is used in tonics, toothpaste, abdominal medicines and to sooth gum and mouth sores.

Nautical Time: Referring to designated time zones around the Earth. The United States of America contains several time zones beginning on the east coast with Eastern Standard Time (EST).

Neutron star: Originally thought to be stars with a radius of 5-15 kilometers and a density similar to that of packed nuclear matter, it is believed radiation escapes only from the north and south poles of the rotating stars.

Nova: In ancient times, a star not previously visible due to distance or magnitude suddenly appeared when it exploded. Citizens thought it was a new star and called it nova, meaning new. The light eventually dimmed.

Opposition: Refers to the position of a planet beyond the Sun when the whole surface facing Earth is illuminated by the Sun.

Orbit: The path a natural or manmade satellite takes around another object, such as the orbit of the Earth around the Sun.

Osiris: Legendary son of the earth god "Geb" and humane sovereign of Egypt. Osiris created the first local and national

laws with wisdom, creating the Egypt civilization and induc-
ing men to give up cannibalism.

Persia: Expected the motions of objects in the sky to announce
the birth of the first three messiahs for the Zoroastrian religion.

Pharaohs: Rulers of Egypt believed to be descendents of
Osiris; upon death their soul was supposed to rise and become
a living star in the sky.

Plane: Flat area or line, such as the Ecliptic Plane extending
in all directions from the Suns' equator.

Planet: A celestial body revolving around a star, such as the
Earth orbiting the Sun.

Plasma: The fourth state of matter after solid, liquid and gas.
Plasma consists of very high energy gases found in fusion reac-
tors, the sun, and other stars.

Precession of the Poles: The axis of the Earth wobbles as
the Earth's rotation slows. One wobble, or precession, takes
25,000-years.

Priests: Ancient priests and temple servants numbered up
to 5,000 per temple. The exalted were very learned men in
mathematics and astronomy. Advisors to leaders/kings, they
offered to their gods mutton, fish, bread, flour, cakes, butter,
fruit, honey and beer.

Regeneration: To reform or be reborn.

Retrograde motion: When an outer planet appears to move
backwards.

Revolution: A move in orbit around another object; such as when Earth orbits or revolves around the Sun.

Rotation: Spinning around the axis.

Shamash: A Babylonian name for the Sun.

Sheba: Ancient region of Southern Arabia later colonized as Ethiopia; currently known as Yemen.

Sirius: The "dog star" in the constellation Canis; the brightest star in our night sky.

Solstice: The days in the calendar when the Sun is at the highest (summer solstice) or lowest (winter solstice) in altitude in a hemisphere.

Statue gems: Precious minerals attached to statues of Elam and Babylonian gods.

Sumer: Refers to the ancient Sumerian civilization of southern Mesopotamia dating to 3500 B.C. Most likely destroyed by the salts of excessive irrigation.

Supernova: The explosion of a massive star.

Transit: To move in front of another object; such as when Venus or Mercury pass in front of the Sun.

Zenith: The point directly above your head that, when you are standing, extends out into space.

Zodiac: The twelve constellations behind the ecliptic used by Babylonians to create personal horoscopes. NASA recently added another constellation to the list to make the total thirteen.

Zoraster: A Persian prophet; founder of the religion Zoroastrianism.

References

Abell, G.O., Morrison, D., Wolff, S.C . *Exploration of the Universe*. Saunders College Publishing. Philadelphia. 1987.

Alter, D., Cleminshaw, C.H., Phillips, J.H. *Pictorial astronomy*. Crowell. New York. 1974.

Aveni, A. *Empires of Time*. Basic Books. Harper Collins. New York. 1989.

Avi-Yonah. M. *Introducing Archaeology.* Cassell. London. 1973.

Bacon, E. *Archaeology: Discoveries in the 1960's*. Praeger Publishers. New York.1971.

Bailey, J. The god-Kings & the Titans: the New World Ascendancy in Ancient Times. St. Martin's Press. New York. 1973

Begley, S. The Christmas Star. *Newsweek*. D. 30. 118: 54-5. 1991.

Binford, L.R. In Pursuit of the Past: Decoding the Archaeological Record. Thames and Hudson. New York. 1983.

Brecher, K., Feirtag, M. *Astronomy of the ancients*. MIT Press. Cambridge.1979.

Caes, C.J. *Studies in Starlight: Understanding Our Universe*. TAB Books, Inc. Blue Ridge Summit. 1988.

Calvin, W. *How the Shaman Stole The Moon*. Bantam Books. New York. 1991.

Camp, L. *Great Cities of the Ancient World*. Doubleday & Co., Garden City, New York. 1972.

Carmody, D.L. The Oldest God: Archaic Religion Yesterday & Today. Abingdon. Nashville. 1981.

Castiglioni, M., Chatterjee, S. P., Gerlach, A. C., Koeman, C., Libault, A., Thackwell, D., Voskuil, R., Watanabe, A.*Rand McNally: The International Atlas*. Rand McNalley & Company. Chicago. 1969.

Ceram, C.W. *Hands On the Past*. Alfred A. Knopf. New York. 1966.
Chaisson, ZE., McMillan, S. *Astronomy Today*. Prentice Hall, Englewood Cliffs, New Jersey. 1993.

Champdor, A. *Babylon*. Elek Books. London. 1958.
Charles-Piccard, G. Larousse Encylopedia of Archeology.

G.P. Putnam & Sons. New York. 1972.
Clark, D.H. *The Cosmos From Space.* Crown Publishers. New York. 1987.

Cleere, G. Stargazing Notes for April 1988. *News! From the Naval Observatory.* Pp. 1-2. 1988.

Cleere, G. The Moon and Sun. *News! From the Naval Observatory.* P. 1 1988, June.

Cleere, G. The Beginning of spring. *News! From the Naval Observatory.* Pl.2 . March. 1989.

Cleere, G. Leap Second Coming. *News! From the Naval Observatory.* P. 2. October. 1989.

Conenau, G. *Everyday Life in Babylon & Assyria.* W.W. Norton & Company, Inc. New York. 1966.

Cottrell, L. *Lady of the Two Lands: Five Queens of Ancient Egypt.* Gobbs-Merrill Company, Inc. Indianapolis. 1967.

DeYoung, J., Hildton, J. "Star of Bethlehem." *Sky & Telescope.* April. 73. 357-358. 1987.

Dixon, R. *Dynamic Astronomy.* Prentice Hall, Englewood Cliffs. 1989.

Dreyer, J. A History of Astronomy from Thales to Kepler. Heath. 1953.

Dunn, R., Abrahamse, D., Davison, G., Farmer, E., Garvey, J., McNeill, W., Schillings, 3D., Victor, D. *A World History: Links Across Time & Place.* McDougal, Littell & Company. 1988.
Emiliani, C. *The Scientific Companion.* John Wiley & Sons. New York. 1988.

Evans, D. *The Wrong Way Comet and Other Mysteries of Our Solar System.* TAB Books.1 Blue Ridge Summit. Pennsylvania. 1992.

Frazier, K. *Solar system.* Time Life Books. Morristown. 1985.

Fairservis, W. Jr. *Egypt, Gift Of The Nile.* MacMillan Company. New York. 1963.

Gilbert, C., Ed. *Larousse Encyclopedia of Archaeology.* The Hamlyn Group. Norwich. 1972.

Glutting, S. "The Moon." *News! From the Naval Observatory.* P. 1. March. 1990.

Grant, M. *The History of Ancient Israel.* Charles Schribner & Sons. N.Y. 1984.

Hamblin, D.J. *The First Cities.* Time Life Books. New York. 1973.

Hammond Historical World Atlas: Volume One, Volume Two. Hammond Inc. Newsweek.1971.

Hapsgood, C.H. *Maps of the Ancient Sea Kings.* Turnstone Books. London. 1979.

Hawkins, G. *Beyond Stonehenge.* Harper & Row. New York. 1973.

Hawkins, G. *Mindsteps To The Cosmos.* Harper & Row. New York. 1983.

Hawkins, G. "Stargazers of the Ancient World:. *Yearbook of Science & the Future.* Encylopaedia Britannica. Chicago. 1975.

Hicks, J. *The Persians.* Time Life Books. New York. 1973.

Hay. J. *Ancient China.* Henry Z. Walch, Inc. New York. 1974.

Hodges, H. *Technology in the Ancient World.* Alfred A. Knopf. New York. 1970.

Holy Bible, People's Parallel Large Print Edition, King James Version and The Living Bible. Tyndale House Publishers, Inc. Wheaton. 1981.

Hoyle, F. *Astronomy.* Doubleday & Co., Inc. Garden City. 1962. Huber, R.V. *The Bible Through the Ages.* Readers Digest. New York. 1996.

Kraeling, E. *Rand McNally Bible Atlas.* Rand McNally & Company. New York. 1952.

Kramer, S. & Editors of Time Life Books. *Great Ages of Man: Cradle of Civilization.* Time Inc. New York. 1967.

Krupp, E. "Ancient Watchers of the Sky." *1980 Science Year.* World Book Science Annual. Chicago: World Book – Childcraft International. 9B-113. 1979.

Krupp, E. *Archaeoastronomy and the Roots of Science.* AAAS Selected Symposium 71. Westview Press. Boulder, CO 1984. Krupp, E.C. *Echos of the Ancient Skies: The Astronomy of Lost Civilizations.* Harper & Row Publishers, Inc. New York, New York. 1983.

Krupp, E. *Skywatchers, Shamans & Kings*. John Wiley & Sons, Inc. New York. 1997.

Lamsa, G.M. *Holy Bible From the Ancient Eastern Text*. HarperCollins Publishers, New York. 1968.

Lehner, E. *Symbols, Signs & Signets*. Dover Publications, Inc. New York. 1996.

Ley, W. *Watchers of the Skies*. Viking Press. New York. 1969.
Lyons, A. *Predicting The Future*. Harry N. Abrams, Inc. New York. 1990.

MacQuitty, W. *Abu Simbel*. G.P. Putnam's Sons. New York. 1965.

Mahdy, C. Mummies, Myth and Magic in Ancient Egypt. Thames & Hudson. Spain. 1989.

Margueron, J.C. *Mesopotamia*. Nagel Publishers. Geneva. 1965.

Medford, Ron. Satellite Laser Ranging System To Be activated At U.S. Naval Observatory's Station in Miami. *News! From the Naval Observatory*. Pp. 1-2. March. 1988.

Mendelssohn, K. *The Riddle of the Pyramids*. Praeger Publishers. New York. 1974.

Meyers, E., & Strange, J. Archaeology, the Rabbis, and Early Christianity: The Social & Historical Setting of Palestinian Judaism and Chrtianity. Parthenon Press. Nashville. 1981.

Miller, R. (Ed.). *The Complete Gospels: Annotated Scholars Version*. Polebridge Press Book. Harper. San Francisco. 1994.

Molnar, M. "The Coins of Antioch". *Sky & Telescope*. January 1992. 37-39. 1992.

Molnar, M. *The Star of Bethlehem*. Rutgerts University Press. New Brunswick. New Jersey. 2000.

Moore, P. *Astronomers; Stars*. W. Norton, New York. 1989.

North, J. *The Norton History of Astronomy & Cosmology*. W.W. Norton & Co., New York, N.Y. 1995.

Pasachoff, J. *Journey Through the Universe*. Saunders College Publishing. Orlando. 1994.

Paul, John II, His Holiness *Crossing The Threshold of Hope*. Alfred A. Knopf. New York. 1995.

Pickering, J. *Asterisks*. Dodd, Mead & Co. New York. 1964.

Ronan, C. *Lost Discoveries*. Bonanza Books. New York. 1976.

Ryan, K. "What Would You Like to Know?" *Catholic Digest*. 58. 3. Pp. 126-7. 1994.

Rubincam, D. "Does an Ancient Jewish Amulet Commemorate the Conjunction of 2 B.C.?" *Skeptical Inquirer*. 17. 78-80. 1992.

Sagan, C. *Cosmos*. Random House. New York. 1980.

Scarre, C. *Smithsonian Timelines of the Ancient World*. Dorling Kindersley. New York. 1993.

Schaefer, B. "Heavenly Signs." *New Scientist*. December 21/28. 48-51. 1991.

Schafer, E.H. Editor. *Great Ages of Man; Ancient China*. Time Life Books, New York. 1967.

Showker, K. *Fodor's Egypt: 1984*. New York: Fodor's Travel Guides. 1983.

Sinnott, R. "Computing the Star of Bethlehem". *Sky & Telescope.* December. 72. 632 – 635. 1986.

Snow, T.P. Essentials of the Dynamic Universe, An Introduction To Astronomy. 2nd Edition. West Publishing. St. Paul. 1987.

Social Science Staff of Educational Research Council of America. *The Human Adventure: Ancient Civilization*. Allyn & Bacon, Inc. Boston. 1975.

Stephenson, F., Clark, D. "Ancient Astronomical Records from the Orient". *Sky & Telescope.* 53. 2. 84-91. 1977.

Talcott, R. "A Burst of Discovery: The First Days of Supernova 1987A." *Astronomy.* Vol. 15. No.6. p.90-95. 1987.

Thomas, G. *Rediscovering Christmas*. Tidings. Nashville. 1954.
Thompson, R.C. editor. Volume II. The Reports of The Magicians and Astrologers of Nineveh and Babylon. Luzac & Co. London. 1990.

Thompson, R. C. editor. *Luzac's Semitic Text and Translation Series*. Volume VI: The Cuneiform Texts. Luzac & Co. London 1990.

Thuan Trinh Xuan *The Secret Melody and Man Created the Universe*. Oxford University Press. New York. 1995.

Waters, T.R. *Planets: A Smithsonian Guide*. Macmillan. New York. 1995.

Weiss, N. *Sky Watchers of Ages Past.*_Houghton Mifflin Co. Boston 1982.

White, J. *Ancient Egypt: Its Culture and History.*_Dover Publications. New York. 1970.

Who's Who In the Bible. Pleasantville NY: Readers Digest Association, Inc. 1994.

Wilkinson, R. *Symbol & Magic In Egyptian Art*. Thomas & Hudson, Ltd. London. 10, 17, 20, 23, 29,66,158. 1994.

Wilson, C. *Starseekers*. Doubleday & Company. New York. 1980.

Wilson, D. *The New Archaeology*. Alfred A. Knopf. New York. 1975.

Worlds Last Mysteries. New York: Readers Digest. 1978.
Zim, H., Baker, R. *Stars*. Golden Press. New York. 1975.

Zimmerman, L. Heads & Tales of Celestial Coins. *Sky & Telescope.*_89. 3. Pp. 28-29. 1995.

Index

India: 55, 58, 92
Indian: xvii, xviii, 32, 52, 70
Iran: 54, 55
Iraq: 26, 43
Iesus: 58, 118
Ishtar: 35, 52

Jahshua: 58
Japanese: xvii
Jehoshua: 58
Jerusalem: 4, 5, 94
Jeshua: 58
Jesu: 58
Jesus: ix, xi, xii, xv, xviii, 2, 4,
    9, 13, 21, 38, 40, 42, 43-45,
    51, 53, 56-58, 62, 63,
    65-69, 71, 72, 83, 85, 90,
    94, 96-98, 101, 104-106
Joshua: 58
Judea: xiv, 4, 5, 7, 11, 38, 57,
    60, 62, 64, 70
Jupiter: 32, 39-42, 52, 57, 58,
    69

Kaimann: 42
Karnack: 46
Kedar: 86
Kronos: 42

Lahmu: 94
Lapis Lazuli: 53, 89, 90
Latitude: xiii, 98, 99, 101, 103
Lehem: 94

Leo: 59
Longitude: xiii, 99, 100
Luminous: 20, 28
Luna: 27

Magi: xii, 53, 70, 98
Magician: xii, 70
Magnitude: 104, 108
Marduk: 52
Mars: 32, 37-40, 58-69, 74-83,
    103, 108
Matthew: 4-6, 8, 10, 85, 94
Medina: 86
Magalith: 55
Mekong: 45
Messiah: 53, 58
Messier, Charles: xvi, xvii
Micah: 94
Midian: 86
Middle East: xii, 26
Migdal-Edar: 94
Milky Way: 19, 28
Moon: xi, xii, svii, 16, 18-23,
    25-28, 31, 34, 35, 38, 40,
    41, 52, 53, 57-65, 67-70,
    73-78, 81, 82, 87, 90, 97,
    103, 104, 107, 108
Moonshine: 20
Mustaabarru-Mutany: 39
Myrrh: 9

Naburianna: 25
Nadir: 14

Sol: 28
Soviet Caucasus: 43
Stars: xi-xiii, xv, 2, 4-6, 14,
  16, 18, 23, 24, 28, 29, 31,
  35, 36, 43, 44, 47, 50, 51,
  55-57, 59, 66, 68-70, 80,
  83, 87, 95, 97, 99, 103,
  105-107
Sumer: 54
Sumerian: 32, 35, 52, 54
Sun: xi, xii, 2, 16, 18, 19-25,
  27-29, 31, 32, 35, 37,
  40, 41-44, 46, 48, 50-54,
  57-82, 87-90, 95, 97, 98,
  103, 104, 109
Supernova: xi, xv, xvii

Taurus: xvi, xx, 35
Titan: 42
Thebes: 89
Time, Astronomical: 103
Time, Civil: 103
Time, Clock: 19
Time, Greenwich: 116
Time, Local: xiii
Time, Nautical: 103
Time, Star: 103, 104, 108
Tower of the Flock: 94, 95
Tutankhamen: 50, 88, 89

Universe: xii, xiiii, xiv, xviii, 24,
  28, 47, 53, 60-62, 67, 68, 88,
  93-96, 98, 100, 106, 109
Ur-Nammu, King: 26
Ursa Minor: 16, 47
United States Navel
  Observatory: 19

Valley of the Kings: 89
Venus: xvii, 32, 34, 35, 39,
  40, 52, 53, 57-63, 65-69,
  74-83, 102, 103, 105
Waning: 26
Waxing: 26
Wisemen: xii, xiv, 2, 4, 25, 43,
  44, 46, 53, 70, 83, 85, 87,
  98

Yang: 32
Yang Wei-Te: xv
Yemen: 86
Yeshu: 58
Yuz Asaf: 58
Yuza: 58

Zanesville Art Center: 92
Zenith: 11-13
Zoraster: 53
Zoroastrian: 53, 118, 121

A Note to My Readers

I hope you enjoyed reading the facts about the Christmas star events. That I found a sequence of ten events occurring in a logical order amazed me as I studied the ancient astronomy symbolism and interpretations. According to what the ancient astronomers believed, the celestial events accurately predicted the birth of the greatest God of all, Jesus Christ. Since movements of the Sun, Moon, stars and planets are mathematically precise, accuracy of the computer calculations was not a worry. It was satisfying to have the information confirmed by other programs.

-Irene Baron

Made in the USA
Charleston, SC
05 March 2014